ANNE P

SEAWEED AND SAFFRON CAKE

★

Memories of a
Cornish Childhood

★

THE WOOLMEAD PRESS

PUBLISHED IN 2001 BY
THE WOOLMEAD PRESS
33 WOOLMEAD AVENUE
LONDON NW9 7AX

ISBN 0 9540965 0 9

Designed by Fred Price
Printed by Octoprint, Chippenham

Illustrations by Edna Wallace

Photographs between pages 16-17
are the property of the author

Contents

1. Beginnings

My first memory is of being wheeled along by my Father in a folding pushchair. It had a seat made of Axminster carpet rather like that found in the halls of cheap hotels. We were walking along a cliff path when one of the wheels got caught in a rabbit hole and I was suddenly thrown out onto the ground. I was not hurt or particularly frightened, and there was a lovely smell of wild thyme under my nose. I was two and a half years old, and that is my earliest recollection.

The next memory is of a small terrier called Fifie. We were looking after a parrot which belonged to an Army friend of my Father's who was serving abroad. This bird had the horrid habit of imitating its owner's voice so well that the poor dog was always fooled when it called out, 'Come on Fifie, come on, walks girl!'. She would rush down the stairs to the front door, always to be disappointed. I can remember my Mother putting a cover over the cage, and telling me to comfort the dog. I loved the feel of Fifie's warm little body against mine as I gave her biscuits out of a jar kept on the sideboard in the dining room. Perhaps I enjoyed this because I usually managed to eat a biscuit myself, in spite of having been told they were only for the dog.

I was born on the 3rd May 1917. I cannot think it was a very auspicious day on which to put in an appearance. It was the time when the most appalling war the modern world had ever seen was at its worst. My parents were hoping for a son. They already had two daughters, but the second girl had died very suddenly of meningitis only six weeks before my birth, and my poor Mother had been shattered by her loss.

To face the birth of another child at that time must have been very hard for her, as I turned out to be another girl, and an ugly baby at that. There is no doubt about my looks, I have seen photographs, and my older sister was a very pretty child with dark eyes and long black hair.

However, in spite of what may have not been a good beginning, I have on the whole had a long and happy life.

I was born in St Albans, and christened in the beautiful Abbey where my parents had been married six years before. Apparently my name was a problem. Only male names had been considered, and I was told later that it was not until we were all in a taxi on our way to the Church that my godmother asked quite reasonably, 'What are you going to call her?'

The result was a hurried agreement on Annette – a name I detested all my childhood, partly because it was 'foreign'. Perhaps this was an early indication of a life-long anti-European stance, something which has not become unfashionable!

The world I was born into was going through an extraordinary time of change. The settled Edwardian England had gone forever, the population had been decimated by the slaughter going on in many theatres of War; 'Theatres of War', what an extraordinary way to describe the battle scenes reported in the newspapers every day, accompanied by the ever-increasing list of casualties printed in heavy black type. The social pattern was changing, and class distinction was never to be the same again.

But my parents had met and started their married life in a secure world and they had two good years before the outbreak of War changed everything. They had met at a dance in the Town Hall, given by a mutual friend. At the dance, my Father told a friend, 'Look at that girl in the cream satin dress. I'm going to marry her.'

This he did a year later in 1912. Anyway, that was the story he told me, and Mother never contradicted him. He was thirty-four and she was only twenty, so there was a considerable difference in their ages, but this did not seem to be a problem and I think they had a long and happy marriage.

My Father was a Gloucester man, his Father was a Doctor and Surgeon in the town. In those days you could be both a physician and surgeon, and he had won a Gold Medal for surgery in his last year at

Barts Hospital, and he operated at the infirmary in Gloucester. I should think the surgery done there on poor patients was pretty primitive, but I was told he was a kind and popular man, much loved by the slum-dwellers of the Cathedral district. I still have a small silver inkstand presented to him by the poor of the parish for the care he gave them during the typhoid epidemic of 1865. There were four sons and three daughters in my Father's family, but the early death of my Grandfather at the age of fifty-six left my Grandmother to bring up a family in fairly straitened circumstances. My Father was only sixteen but he had to leave the Crypt Grammar School and go to work in a wine-merchant's business. This was considered suitable for a gentleman's son – trade was out of the question, but publishing, bookselling and wine selling were not thought of as 'trade'; they were on the fringes of the professions.

When my Grandfather died the eldest son was already studying medicine at Guy's Hospital, and the younger ones remained at school until they too were old enough to go to work. I never knew what happened to my Aunts, except to hear they died young. So for several years the family all lived at home with their Mother in the house where my Grandfather had had his surgery.

My Mother's family lived in St Albans. Her Father was a prosperous hat manufacturer, specialising in straw boaters and fine panama hats. They lived in a large house on St Peter's Street, and seemed to have had quite a social life. Mother told us of large dinner parties and dances held in people's homes. She and her two sisters had a busy round of entertaining and being entertained after they left school. When her Father died, my Mother was only nineteen, but the family was well provided for and my maternal Grandmother had no financial worries.

After my parents were married, my Father took over the management of the hat factory. My Grandmother had had difficulties in running the business after her husband's death, and it seemed a good arrangement to 'keep it in the family', so to speak. Though how having been a wine-merchant could have been in any way useful in the making of hats has always been a mystery to me, he apparently did well and the business continued to prosper.

My parents lived in a pretty house, which had once been a vicarage, on the edge of the town. They had servants: a cook, housemaid, gardener and a woman for 'the rough', and when my sister arrived a year later, a Nanny.

But life was not so pleasant for long.

By the time I was born in 1917 they had moved to a smaller house in the town; there was no gardener; Father's factory was making soldiers' caps instead of elegant boaters. He was a volunteer constable, and Mother managed with a cook general, no other servants, and she did part-time work as a V.A.D. Many of their young friends and relatives had been killed or wounded, and all my uncles were at the Front.

I remember as I grew up trying to understand how things had been before the War, how much of grown-up conversation seemed to be about a halcyon time which had gone forever. We had one shell-shocked cousin who visited us from time to time, who was not able to read aloud to me. This was something I assumed all grown-ups did if you asked them politely, and I could not understand his blank looks when I showed him one of my picture books.

When the War ended, people tried to go back to the way things had been before 1914. Quite impossible, of course, but my early childhood was somewhat blighted by their efforts. The amount of snobbery was ridiculous, and it applied to all classes. One knew certain people or one didn't. I was always being told that 'one' doesn't do this or that, when I behaved in a way unacceptable to adults.

For years I wondered who 'one' was. How did one know it was not right to play with the charlady's little girl when she came to the house with her Mother? Why did one always insist that you replied, 'Very well, thank you' to any enquiry as to how you were, when in fact you might be feeling sick or miserable? Our servants were as snobbish as we were. Cook always called the gardener Mr Pate, though they had been children in school together. She would not eat her dinner at the same table as the woman who came to do the laundry and rough work.

Of course things did gradually change as the horrors of the war receded, and we reverted in some degree to the pre-war situation. Servants reappeared; we had a cook, housemaid and Nanny. Mother resumed making calls on neighbours, leaving appropriate cards at each address. My elder sister went to day school, and I spent most of my time with Nanny or in the kitchen with cook.

Cook's name was Ethel. She was a tall, skinny woman with a red face and wispy hair, a lovely person, and unlike many grown-ups did not mind answering questions – always providing I did not get under her feet, as she used to say. I spent hours sitting at the kitchen table watching her at work and plying her with questions.

The best days were when she was making cakes for my Mother's bridge parties. These needed icing, and I was allowed to run my finger round the bowl and lick the sweet mixture. At the run-up to Christmas, everyone had a turn at mixing the puddings which were made early in October. Even my Father would join in this ceremony, and drop silver threepenny pieces into the bowl for some lucky person to find on Christmas day.

Ethel used to have a conference with Mother every morning to settle the menu for the day, and lists would be made to go to the grocer or butcher for the items we needed. These were delivered by cheerful boys on bicycles with huge wicker baskets on front. Even a packet of tea was delivered in those days, and a monthly account for each shop was kept in a coloured notebook which was hung on a hook on the kitchen dresser.

One item of food which was special to winter was muffins. These were brought by the muffin man who came down our road on Friday afternoons, and I never hear a handbell being rung without recapturing the excitement when we heard him coming. We were allowed to go to the gate with a white napkin to collect the muffins. He carried them on a tray balanced on a sort of round cushion on top of his cap. They tasted wonderful – like nothing I have ever eaten since. Warm, soft, thick and slightly salted, toasted in front of a coal fire and filled with butter, on foggy winter afternoons they were something to remember.

Another regular who passed down our street was the lamplighter. He came at dusk and carried a long pole with a hook on the end. With this he pulled at the chain hanging from the top of the post and the tiny gas flame sprang into life, making pools of light which lit up pavements glistening with rain or sparkling with frost.

When I was four, my younger sister was born. I didn't have any idea that Mother was having a baby, and it came as a complete surprise when, having spent the night at my Grandmother's, I went home and saw the new arrival. I cannot remember being pleased or sorry. It just seemed to me to be one more inexplicable thing that grown-ups did.

The immediate result for me was that I was expected to do much more for myself. Nanny had less time for me, being taken up with looking after the new arrival. Some of the developments were agreeable, like not being too carefully supervised when washing my hands before meals; others not so good, as when I needed help doing up my shoelaces.

It did, however, have one very good outcome. I spent much more time with my Father. I think he realised I was feeling a bit neglected, and he began to take me about with him whenever possible. We formed a lifelong closeness, and he taught me many things which stood me in good stead in later life. One place he used to take me to was the Tennis Club. He was an excellent player and had won several tournaments before the war; of course, it was an entirely amateur sport in those days. While he was playing, I was left to wander among the spectators, and to chat to those who condescended to talk to me. I remember one afternoon when I was talking to an old gentleman called Montague. He was wearing a large panama hat and carried a silver-headed cane. He suddenly asked me, 'Would you like an ice-cream?'

Of course, I replied that I would. He told me to go to the refreshment tent and buy one. He gave me the money, and although I was surprised that he did not want one for himself I soon returned to the seat beside him with a large strawberry ice. Not, of course, in a cone, but on a glass plate, with two lovely fan-shaped wafers sticking out of the top. The old gentleman seemed pleased to see me enjoying it, and after I thanked him again, he removed the large cigar which he was smoking, and asked me if I would like another!

I was somewhat taken aback by this because I was never allowed more than one ice-cream, and that only on very special occasions. However, it seemed too good an offer to refuse, so I accepted, and trotted off to get another. The lady in the tea tent seemed a little surprised at my asking for a second, so I told her that Mr Montague had asked me to buy it, almost implying it was for him. This is the first time I can remember being what is now known as 'economical with the truth', and I had some twinges of conscience about it. However, I ate the ice and there were no dire consequences.

Another thing I did with my Father was enjoy books. He was an excellent reader, and I knew all the Beatrix Potter books by heart long before I could read them for myself. How exciting it was to wait for the best parts – for Squirrel Nutkin's tail to be pulled off by Mr Brown; Peter Rabbit escaping from Mr MacGregor; and the Bad Mice smashing everything in the dolls' house. I loved *The Pied Piper* with its wonderful rhymes. I cried over *Black Beauty*, and shivered at *Grimms' Fairy Tales*. Long after I could read myself, I would curl up in an armchair and beg Father to read to me.

I can't remember when I began to read or write. I had no formal teaching until I was nearly six and went to a little Dame's school. We all painted and used crayons and pencils. Cutting out was a great pastime, and making scrap-books of all kinds of collections kept me busy. We collected cigarette cards, and pressed flowers and ferns. We played lots of table games, Ludo, Halma, card games like Snap and Happy Families, so I think we learned some number skills in that way. My early education was strictly on the practical side, mostly how to *do* things rather than intellectual knowledge.

My early years were full of interest. I don't remember grown-ups being very prominent other than family and Nanny. Children lived apart from adults, and never joined in their social life except at Christmas and very special family gatherings. This protected us from the worries and difficulties of the world. We were not aware of business being bad, or difficulties between parents. I am sorry for children today who are so often burdened with such knowledge from far too early an age.

However, there was one aspect of social life which was a worry to me: parties! These took place in people's homes or sometimes in the Town Hall ballroom if it was a big gathering.

The getting ready was a torture to me, though my sister Rosemary loved it. One had to stand still while hair was curled. Then we got into layers of clothing. First a flannel petticoat, then a cotton one which had lace round the bottom which had been goffered and starched so stiffly that it cut into the back of your legs when you sat down. Finally the party frock, with a wide sash tied at the back. This inevitably would wind its way round to the front during lively games and be very difficult to get straight. To cap it all, a bow on top of one's head, which I felt sure made me look ridiculous.

I hated the games like Postman's Knock or Musical Chairs, because I was always too slow to win them. Tea was not too bad: cakes, jellies and ice-cream, but always the lurking worry that you might spill something down your frock. However, at the end there might be Roger de Coverley, a rowdy country dance in which one could really let off steam. Finally, being taken to say 'thank you' to the hostess, and then thankfully wrapped up and bundled into a taxi and taken home to the security of one's own bed.

Parties finished for me when my Father's business took us away from St Albans to live in the West Country.

2. Move to Cornwall

WHEN I was five years old we moved to Cornwall. It was 1922, and then began an entirely different chapter in my life.

For some reason which was never clear to me, my Father had become the manager of a wine merchants business in Plymouth. Perhaps the decline in the wearing of hats, particularly those like boaters and panamas had resulted in the decline of the factory he ran in St Albans, I only know the factory was closed, and we moved from a suburban house in town to the country, to a bungalow in a tiny village on the south coast of Cornwall. I have often wondered why my parents chose to live there. It was a complete contrast to the surroundings of their previous life. I wish now that I had asked my Father about this, but I never did. Children did not enquire about things like that when I was young. Perhaps one of the saddest things about old age is the realisation of how little one knows about things which happened earlier, and then suddenly it is too late. There is no one left to ask.

Whatever the reason for our move we all loved our new home, and soon became part of village life, though it is true that we were not completely accepted by the locals for some time. The Cornish were, still are I think, suspicious of people who came from 'up-a-long'. Everyone was a foreigner who came from the other side of the Tamar river. This did not apply so much to visitors, tourists as they are called today. They were fair game for reaping financial benefit. But for people who moved into the Duchy to live it was different. I know my Father said he only felt he had been fully accepted when he won a prize at the Annual Flower Show some years after we had gone to live in Cornwall.

The village lay on a narrow strip of land below rounded hills, about a hundred feet above the shore. The road which led into the village turned suddenly sharply to the right round a hairpin bend, displaying the whole expanse of the Channel beyond. Beside the bend set back from the road was the first house, the Manor. It stood in a large well treed garden and was occupied by an elderly lady who was the only person who might have been thought of as the Lord of the Manor. She owned very little land, but her family had lived there for years so she was accepted as the senior person to be consulted in any serious village matter.

At the bottom of the hill as the road flattened out was a tiny cottage. It stood beside a stream on a path called Bottle Lane. This stream provided the water used by the woman who lived in the cottage, Mrs Smith. She was the local washerwoman and a formidable figure. A large stout woman, always dressed in black. She invariably wore a bonnet, the style of which varied with the season. Straw in the summer with a flower or two pinned on rather haphazardly, in the winter black velvet which had tarnished with age to the colour of old bronze.

She had a husband who scratched a living growing potatoes on various little plots round the cottage. These were fertilised by the seaweed which he carried up from the beach in autumn in a huge basket strapped to his back. Mr Smith was a dour man who seldom spoke to anyone if he could help it, certainly not to children, but his wife was altogether different. She always greeted one in a friendly way.

'Well my pretty, what be you up to today?' she would ask.

She had a donkey which was usually the reason for my visiting Bottle Lane. It drew a small flat cart in which she used to deliver the laundry round the village. Like any other animal it was a magnet to me. I loved going into the dark little cave in the side of the hill where it was stabled, and feeling its velvety nose which nuzzled my hand as I fed it the milky sow thistles which grew beside the stream.

Beyond Bottle Lane the road wandered down a small hill past the austere Weslyan Chapel perched on the hillside down to a widening out to Broard's farm yard on the right and the village shop on the left.

This was the centre of village life. The place where everyone met to exchange news and gossip, to enjoy the small local scandals. The variety of goods it supplied was astonishing. Sides of bacon hung from the rafters, beside paraffin lamps and coils of rope. Behind the shop were sheds which accommodated stock and it was remarkable what

Downderry (East)

Downderry (West)

Bottle Gate, Downderry

Downderry

Seaton Valley, Downderry

Seaton, The Sands, Downderry

Shag Rock, Downderry

could be found there. Items like bicycle pumps, a jar of ginger left over from Christmas, washers for taps, and skeins of knitting wool.

No one was ever in a hurry to be served, and nothing was pre-packed, shopping was a very leisurely affair.

Sugar was weighed out into blue bags, biscuits into white ones. Butter was sharply patted into shape with wooden pats and finished off with a mould which left a pattern of a rose on its surface. Bacon rashers were sliced from the sides taken down from the ceiling and eggs counted out from a big brown bowl standing on the wooden counter.

The Post Office was in a corner behind a wire grill. On the shelf in front of the grill was a very large inkpot. Attached to this was a fearsome pen which spattered alarmingly when used to obey the order, 'Sign Here'. This did not happen very often as there were no payouts, no pension books, child allowances or invalidity benefits to be collected then. The Post Office business was mainly stamps, telegrams, and the despatch of a parcel to a son serving in the Navy overseas. No need for security, no one ever held up a Post Office, and everyone knew where *H.M.S. Valiant* was stationed because Mrs Parry's boy was with her in Malta wasn't he?

The women enjoyed their visits to the shop but the children usually avoided it except on Saturdays, pocket money day. Then the deliberations over what to spend those precious pennies on were long and difficult. The usual choice was sweets unless one had some bonus which enabled one to buy a fishing net or perhaps a pocket knife. Generally it came down to the choice between a 'gobstopper' a very large humbug which could be sucked for hours, and even wrapped in a bit of paper and put in a pocket for a later treat, or a triangular paper packet filled with sherbert sucked up through a straw in the corner. There were also licorice bootlaces favoured by the boys but considered by the girls to be 'horrible'.

Beyond the hub of the village the road meandered past the Vicarage, a pretty late Victorian house standing back from the road with a tiny stream flowing through its garden. Next to this was a small white house with a wide porch where Mr Hitchen the lawyer lived. He was reclusive, did not mix in the village, went every day to his office in Liskeard, and had no family.

The next bend disclosed the 'big houses' as they were known. There were three of these and they belonged to families who only came down from London for the holidays. After them more cottages, the Doctor's house and our own long bungalow. That was the extent of our community. We had very few modern facilities. No electricity, no main drainage or gas. There was an excellent water supply but no refuse collection. We had a very good postal service. Our postman was called Jim and he delivered on a pony. It caused quite a stir when in the late thirties he was on the radio programme called *In Town Tonight*. His claim to fame was that he had been the last postman in England to deliver on horseback. Mail in those days was remarkably good. My Grandmother posted a letter every Sunday evening in St Albans and Jim delivered it first thing Monday morning. It had been put on the night train from Paddington, put off at our local station St Germans, picked up by Jim, who sorted his own letters and brought to us. A letter cost a penny and a half in those days.

We were also able to collect letters in the evening by going down to the Post Office at five o'clock. This was an errand we loved doing particularly during the winter. As there was no street lighting you took a hurricane lamp to find your way, and would meet others going on the same errand. Lamps bobbed along the road and one would be met by a friendly, 'Hullo me dear, be you going down for the post then? I'll come along with you then.'

The rest of our shopping needs were met by a butcher who came out with his cart once a week from the local market town, and the fishermen who delivered to the door almost every day.

Telegrams arrived in the form of written messages through the Post Office. There was no boy to deliver them as there were in towns, so anyone would be asked to take them out who might be going near the house of the addressee. Of course the Post Mistress knew the contents, and I remember her saying to me when I picked up a message from my Grandmother which told us of a forthcoming visit, 'Very nice to hear Mrs Scott be coming down next week then.'

For us children the place was a paradise. We had a large garden with a tennis court. There was a tall pine tree with a swing hanging from a high branch. The house had a verandah on three sides and looked out over the Atlantic where it met the Channel. To the east it was bounded by Rame Head which bordered the Plymouth Sound, and to the west was Dodman's Point. This latter was a place of mystery to me when a local fisherman told me the legend that anyone drowned in Dozmary Pool on Bodmin Moor was always swept underground and thrown up at the point. I think this was the first of many legends I heard about Cornwall. The sea was ever present and I learned to love it in all its moods, from calm sparkling summer days, to the hurricane force storms which battered the village in winter and early spring.

The Eddystone lighthouse stood on the horizon. Its friendly beam swept across my bedroom wall at night before the curtains were drawn, and I often fell asleep murmuring the rhythm of its long short, long, long, light.

There was a great deal of shipping and we watched the traffic from our verandah all through the year. There were great Atlantic liners going into Plymouth Sound to disembark their passengers into tenders for the train journey to London, we saw the *Normandie*, the *Mauritania* as they steamed majestically up Channel. Naval vessels coming home from foreign stations to their home port of Devonport, long lines of grey shapes, line astern, such potent symbols of Empire. There was a lot of commercial traffic too, and of these my favourites were the trawlers of the herring fleet with their twinkling lights which stretched across the horizon like a string of pearls.

A winding path ran down from the garden to the beach, at the bottom was a stout sea wall built to rebuff the waves which crashed against the cliff during the storms. Just above the steps which led onto the shore we had a large hut filled with all the paraphanalia of beach life – deck chairs, prawning nets, and buckets and spades; piles of discarded canvas shoes used to climb over the sharp rocks. A blackened kettle used to boil the water for tea over a fire of driftwood gathered from the beach. Along the window ledges was an assortment of shells, and always the smell of decaying seaweed hanging from nails knocked into the wall in a random fashion. Other treasures jostled together, empty crab shells, the green glass balls used to indicate the fishing lines; and our own fishing lines wound round square wooden frames.

There was no unpleasant rubbish on beaches then, no plastic or discarded food containers, all the flotsam and jetsam which came up on shore was eagerly collected by the villagers after every storm.

We were a very self contained community and the villagers did not travel much. Many of them had never been across the Tamar into Devon, and only went to Liskeard for essential business.

When a local lad left home to join the Army it was considered a very daring thing to have done. Tom Pengelly came home on leave and the whole village turned out to see him parading down the street in his grey Guards uniform.

That was the village where I spent my childhood, now obliterated for ever under holiday bungalows and caravan sites.

From a tiny child I had always preferred pets to toys, so when we moved to Cornwall I was delighted to find here was a place with plenty of room for all my feathered and furry friends. I was able to have living creatures as my constant companions throughout my childhood. The only toys I remember treasuring were the pieces of my model farm which I collected for years always hoping for additions at Christmas and birthdays. On wet days I used to set this out on the big table in our playroom, changing it in tune with seasons, always having regard to good farming practices as taught me by our friends in the village. Books were another thing altogether. They were special treasures to be treated with care, into whose wonderful worlds I could escape at will.

My first dog was a present my Father brought home when I was four. He arrived home one day with a basket which he put down on the nursery floor.

When he opened it we saw two tiny Sealyham terrier puppies, one for me and one for my sister. Hers had a black patch over one eye, mine was completely white. This little pup became a member of our household for the next fourteen years. We found out before long that she was completely deaf, possibly because she was so white, but she had lovely brown eyes. Her deafness did not seem to bother her at all. She learned to obey hand signals very quickly, and followed us wherever we went.

Over the years our menagerie was large and varied. The dogs were the most important members and we all had our own.

My Father's labrador Susan was a very important member of the household. She was given to him when she became gun-shy. She was a lovely dog and a good retriever until someone accidentally let off a shotgun close to her head which caused her to become gun-shy and made her useless for future field work. Her owner's loss was our gain. She settled into our household at once and was loved by everyone.

She had a wonderful soft mouth, and one of my Father's favourite tricks was to give her two eggs which she would carry in her mouth and put in to his hand. Her retrieving skills were in great demand when tennis was being played. Father boasted we never lost a ball in the bushes or over the cliff if she was on hand to find it.

Susan also taught us to swim. She naturally loved water and always went to the beach with us. When we were little we used to hang on to her tail and be pulled along. If we ever ventured into deep water she headed us back to safety, and before long we all became good swimmers.

Our other dogs were a motley lot. My Mother had a bulldog called Derry, there were various puppies adopted from time to time because they had no other home to go to, friends' dogs who came to visit when their owners went abroad, and in the summer otterhound puppies which we 'walked' for the local hunt.

There were of course the inevitable tragedies. Many a funeral was held in that part of the garden we called the wild wood. Here was the pine tree from which our swing hung. Dangling gently in summer breezes or lashing wildly in the November gales. Beneath it we buried many precious pets.

White mice carefully wrapped and put in to a shoe box, joined kittens and puppies who failed to make it to adulthood. The graves were watched over by our tortoise Methuselah who wandered about among the bluebells and ferns during the summer and disappeared in September into a pile of leaves for his winter sleep.

There were also panics and comedies caused by our miscellaneous animal family. A disastrous experiment happened one Spring when Father, seeing he would soon have to start mowing the tennis lawn again, was grumbling about the labour necessary. Of course we had no electric mowers in those days and it was a task pushing our old machine cutting the grass ready for play. A neighbour suggested that as the lawn was well fenced we might borrow a few sheep from a local farmer. They would trim it down nicely in a week. The fencing was inspected for security and gates firmly latched before Mr Pengelly promised our friendly ewes who would do the job nicely.

One Saturday they arrived and after a lot of shouting and barking were duly installed on the lawn. For a day they nibbled away happily, watched suspiciously by our dogs who patrolled outside the fence. The calm was shattered early next morning by Lucy our maid rushing in to Father telling him to come at once.

'It's them sheep Sir, thems in the garden having a right go at your vegetables, the cabbages is nearly all gone!'

We all rushed in to the vegetable garden to see a scene of havoc. The amount of damage four hungry ewes can do in a few hours is horrible. The next hour was spent by the whole family getting them back on to the lawn. We fastened the hole they had managed to make in the netting and father rang the farmer telling him to fetch his sheep as soon as possible.

Of course there were other escapees. From time to time rabbits got out of hutches, and bantams out of their run but these did not cause the havoc of the sheep and were usually caught after noisy chases and returned to their lawful dwelling places.

In addition to the larger animals I had a shed in which I kept rabbits, rats, white mice and the occasional hedgehog. Providing their boxes enabled me to develop rough carpentry skills which stood me in good stead in later life.

I never liked keeping birds in cages, but from time to time an injured fledgling, or a seabird picked up on the beach suffering from oil, could be restored to health and released back in to the wild. That was always a small triumph.

3. The Seasons

IT was when we moved to Cornwall that I first became really aware of the seasons. Life in the village all revolved round them, and my year has always been from Autumn as the beginning, more than as for most people January to December.

It was partly because the life of the village was so intimately affected by farming and the agricultural cycle, and partly for us the summer ended holidays and a return to school. There was also the influence of the Church year, which seemed to start anew after Harvest Festival, and took on an impetus with Advent and preparations for Christmas. All these things formed the continuous cycle of life.

The climate was mild on the south coast, and everything was green all year round. I never saw snow until my early teens, though we heard of the wild weather not so far away up on the Bodmin Moors. In our garden mimosa bloomed in February, and we did not have to protect plants against frost. We did, however, have tremendous winter storms. These occurred during late October and November, and often reached hurricane force. The sea became a roaring monster which pounded our beach with huge waves and spray that flew high in the air.

We would don our oilskins and sou'westers and go to the edge of the cliff path to watch the storm. We had to hang on to a bush or fence to avoid being bowled over by the gusts which snatched the breath out of our mouths. After the storm we went down to the shore to look for treasures which might have been thrown up by the waves.

In earlier times, wrecking and smuggling had been carried out by the local people, but by the time I am remembering it had died out, though beachcombing always took place after a storm. Many a good find was dragged into the local houses, particularly supplies of driftwood for firewood.

After the storm, the sun came out and great clouds scudded across the sky, the beach often had a changed appearance. Where before we had played on a sandy stretch, we might find a great bank of shingle, or where there had been a particular rock pool there might be a shelf of sand. I don't think we ever found anything of value, though I did once pick up a little carved wooden figure, which I suppose had been whittled by a sailor during a slow voyage. It was of indeterminate sex, and only had one eye, but I treasured it for years, and made up many a story about its probable origin.

So when I think of the year it all seems to begin with Harvest Festival. This was marked by a special service in Church. The building was decorated with masses of flowers and fruit and vegetables, all piled up round the pulpit and lectern, crowding the window sills, and even up the altar steps. Michaelmas daisies and dahlias jostled with chrysanthemums in the brass vases, and huge vegetable marrows perched precariously on the ledges at the end of the pews. It was always a very joyous occasion, and attended by folk who seldom set foot inside the Church during the year. Some primitive feeling made everyone want to be grateful for the earth's bounty. We sang about ploughing the fields and scattering the good seed with a very real sense of good fortune.

Then there was the Harvest Supper held in the Village Hall. This was a pretty rowdy affair, I gathered from what our parents told us about it. Children did not attend,, for in those days grown-ups had their very adult parties to which the young were not invited. We were, however, sometimes allowed into the Hall to see the preparations: the long trestle tables covered with white cloths; beer barrels set up at the end of the room, beside rows of mugs ready to be filled when the party started. Huge amounts of cooking went on in different houses; great joints, geese and pasties all roasted for the supper. Pies, too, with every kind of fruit. In making these the local women vied to out-do each other, Mrs Greet's blackberry and apple competing with Mrs Pengelly's peach speciality.

After Harvest, work turned toward what might be called 'make and mend'. Buildings and fences were repaired against the winter storms. There was a lovely smell of creosote as wood was waterproofed. Piles of logs stood beside the back doors, and big stones were put on low roofs to hold them firm in the gales.

The fishermen pulled their boats up above the tideline, and stashed oars and lines in huts along the beach. Some of them did go out throughout the winter, but usually only inshore to pick up lobster pots.

Carts went down to the beach to bring back seaweed. This was the main fertiliser used for potato growing and every patch on the cliffside grew potatoes. They were ready early in our part of the world, and vied with the Jerseys for flavour.

Then came Christmas. This was a very exciting time for us. We had been preparing all through Advent, learning carols, making presents and cards. We always made our own cards, and each year wanted to have different colours or themes. Mine, I must say, were not brilliant. I was not artistic, and drawing a camel or a star usually defeated me. One year I boldly decided I would have no more of this art work, and announced my card would simply be 'Happy Christmas' printed on a red card. It worked very well, and was acknowledged to be 'quite good' by my elder sister when I found a packet of stick-on stars in the village shop. These put in the corners gave the cards quite a professional look.

We also made rather awful Christmas decorations out of crêpe paper: rings strung together to make chains, or two or three colours twisted and looped in sorts of garlands. These were were allowed to hang up anywhere except in the drawing room, which was reserved for the Christmas tree.

This always arrived two days before Christmas, and stood bare and majestic. My parents dressed it themselves as a surprise for us children, and on Christmas morning we went in to see it lit up in all its splendour. Underneath were the presents, piled in a heap. Those that had come by post still in their brown wrappings, others in gay papers. I don't know how my Mother managed it, but we never saw sight of a present until that magic moment when we all gathered to see the tree.

I don't remember ever really believing in Father Christmas. He was always a pleasant benign figure of the imagination, but certainly did not come down chimneys. We all hung up our stockings on Christmas Eve, and were awake early to drag them into bed to explore the treasures they held. Very simple things – an orange in the toe of the stockings, then perhaps pencils and crayons, a hair slide, a toy or two new gloves, and something I only ever remember seeing at Christmas, coloured sweets shaped like grapes on a stem. These, although different colours – green, yellow and red – all tasted the same, like blackcurrant. I never knew why!

We did not open our proper presents until after lunch, as the morning was taken up with seeing to all our many pets. Animals must not be neglected because it was a holiday. This chore was followed by Church, then an early lunch after which we settled down to listen to the King's speech, solemn minutes these, and *then* opening the presents. I think we all enjoyed each others' as much as our own. There was much sharing of surprise and joy, only mildly overshadowed by the admonition 'Keep the card carefully, you must remember to write a nice thank-you letter!'

Early in the New Year, exciting things began to happen. Lambs appeared, and on the banks which bordered our deep lanes one could find an early celandine, and tiny violets. Up the valley where trees were a little sheltered, the sticky buds of chestnuts grew shiny and fat, and crocuses sprang up in the grass round the tennis court. We could play on the verandah again without wearing sweaters, or 'woollies' as we called them.

By Easter the primroses were in full flower,, and an annual excursion was to take a picnic up the Hessenford valley to pick a big box full, which we sent to my Grandmother, to decorate the altar in the Abbey in St Albans. We made small bunches and tied them up with wool so as not to cut the stems. The bunches were packed in an old dress box of Mother's, and then taken to the station at St Germans to catch the night train to Paddington. The next day they were sent on to St Albans, and on Easter Saturday put round the altar steps for the Easter celebration.

Spring was always a wonderful time for me. There was new life all round: lambs and calves on the farm, our own hens hatching their chicks, and often kittens belonging to our cat.

As the days grew longer and warmer, we spent more time on the beach, swimming and prawning, and exploring the deep rock pools with their marvellously coloured treasures of anemones and tiny crabs. We spent hours trying to catch a limpet when it relaxed its hold on the rock, and collecting the different kinds of seaweeds which waved in the water as the tide came in. Building a variety of castles out of sand was a pastime more enjoyed by boys than girls; I wonder if that says something about the male character being naturally directed towards engineering? I always felt it was rather a waste to spend so long constructing elaborate structures with their moats and battlements only to see them washed away by the incoming tide.

Summer was a lovely time for us. Visitors came for their annual holiday at the seaside, and every year we greeted old friends who came to stay in houses they rented or in rooms where they were catered for by the village folk.

Summer also meant Carnival and Flower Show time, but these occasions must be kept for another chapter.

4. My Education

MY formal education did not begin until I was nearly six. My elder sister, Rosemary, had been sent to boarding school when we moved to the country, probably because there was no school near us for her to go to daily. She went to the school our Mother had attended in Bexhill, and as far as I can remember she was very happy there. She always came home for the holidays full of the stories of what went on there, in what, to me, was a somewhat mysterious establishment. I looked at her uniform and school trunk with awe, but never wanted to be part of the different world she lived in. The difference in our ages, she was five and a half years older than I, and the fact that she was away from home two thirds of the year, kept us apart. Indeed, I don't think we really got to know each other until we were grown-up and lived apart from home.

The problem of what to do with me must have been quite difficult for my parents. My young sister, Maureen, was only two when we went to Cornwall, so she did not cause any trouble. To begin with, they tried having a help in the house who would also teach me, but the lady who came did not like country life or me, and it was not a success.

It was out of the question that I should go to the local Board School, as state schools were called in those days. It was nearly three miles away, in a slightly larger village than ours. The children of our village walked there every day, carrying a hot pasty wrapped up in a cloth for their dinner, or sometimes a baked potato if times were hard. They walked back in the late afternoon. But of course, for one of the gentry it could not be considered.

Luckily for me, the solution lay in a 'Dame's' school. A lady ran a school in her house not far from where we lived. She took the children whose parents could afford a small fee for education.

I was introduced to Miss Bickford soon after my sixth birthday, and joined her class of eight children. Our ages ranged from five to fourteen, and in the back room of her little terrace house she ruled, not with a rod of iron but with loving kindness, with remarkable results. She was a born teacher, and taught us all basic subjects, from the three 'R's' to Art and History.

We sat round a large table covered with a red chenille cloth. We each had our own books kept in a neat pile in front of us, flanked by a pencil case containing pencils, rubber, ruler and pens. At appropriate times small pots of ink were put in front of us for use in writing. This consisted, to begin with, of making loops between lines and progressing to letters and then joining them together as our skills improved. Considering how much trouble Miss Bickford took to teach me to write properly, I do not understand why my handwriting became so bad; everything else she gave me remained with me for life.

Reading was not difficult. I don't remember exactly when I learned to read, but I know that by five I read to myself whenever given the opportunity, and a book was always my choice of a gift for birthday or Christmas. At school we read a lot of poetry, and learned it by heart. I remember Kipling was a favourite. It was a jingoistic period, and the Empire still something to be proud of. We learned prayers and hymns by heart also, and read the Bible every day, which is certainly the best way to appreciate the English language. Grammar was important, and examples from our brown grammar book remain with me to this day: 'Cain killed Abel' but 'Abel was killed by Cain', is it transitive or intransitive?

The exercise of parsing was the way in which we learned the structure of language. I don't suppose the educationalists of today would approve of small children splitting up sentences and putting the words into the appropriate boxes on a divided page. I loved it, and even now I like prepositions to be in the right place, and detest split infinitives.

In the parlour which was our schoolroom there was a mantlepiece on which stood, or clustered round the frame of the large mirror which surmounted it, cards and letters from old boys and girls. They came from all over the world: from soldiers in India; colonial officers in Burma; tea planters in Ceylon, as it was called then; teachers in Canada and missionaries in China; and many more from other parts of England. Miss Bickford told us all about the writers and they often formed the foundation of our geography lessons. Talking about their news, and looking at the large book of maps spread out before us, we got an idea of many countries and how people lived in remote areas so different from our own surroundings. The UK was not neglected. We had to memorise all the county towns and their rivers. London on the Thames was important, but Bodmin on the Camel seemed to me to be more interesting.

History was enlivened by books like *The Princes in the Tower* and *Lamb's Tales from Shakespeare*; but we tended to concentrate on the Elizabethan period, possibly because the Armada passed our door, so to speak, on its way to meet Drake, who, as we all knew, was playing bowls on Plymouth Hoe at the time.

Music, or rather performing on any instrument, was the one thing even dear Miss Bickford failed to teach me. I did struggle with the piano which stood in her front parlour, but my total ineptitude resulted in her admitting to my Mother that the extra fee which paid for me to achieve even the minimal standard was wasted, and to my relief music was dropped from my curriculum.

Apart from my formal education in the little school, I was taught by everyone round me. Mother taught us practical things like cooking and sewing, and Father showed me the elements of carpentry and gardening. We learned the names of trees, flowers and plants as well as butterflies and insects from daily observation, so our general knowledge was pretty wide. We learned about farming from the village folk, and soon became aware of the seasonal rhythms in that way.

If you wonder what our 'Dame' looked like, I will tell you. She was a little rather round lady. She had white hair very tidily tied into a bun which was on top of her head, and twinkling blue eyes which seldom looked cross. If we misbehaved she reprimanded us in a way which had immediate effect, quite quietly, but very firmly, and always explaining the reason for her displeasure. She always dressed in black, and for Art class she put on a large brown smock, which I am sure was very necessary as we were pretty sloppy with our paints. I was not good at painting, but liked what was known as 'flat drawing'. This was copying a pattern or design, and enlarging it to fit one's paper. I remember Egyptian friezes being rather fun.

So for five years I went to school in a lovely warm atmosphere. I was never bullied or made to feel stupid, and there was no competition between the pupils. You were just expected to do the best you could. I think I was a lucky child having that experience, and I was quite self-confident when later I was sent to a large girls' school and had to cope with thirty in a class and three hundred other girls.

5. Knight's Bus

THERE was no public transport in our village.

The railway station was about four miles inland, so, if you had no car or truck, to leave the village you either had to get a lift, or walk to the station or go in the other direction over the river Tamar to Plymouth.

There was, however, Mr Knight's bus.

Mr Knight was a rather reclusive character who lived in a secluded cottage in the woods up the Hessenford valley. No one knew much about him, he was not a local man, but he was the owner of the bus, or rather 'char-a-banc' as they were called in those days. It was a very ramshackle vehicle which had seen service in France during the War, where it had carried the walking wounded back from the front lines to the first aid posts. It still boasted a red cross on the back, much faded, but still clearly visible. It was not known how it had come into Mr Knight's possession, but the villagers found it very useful to go into town whenever its owner decided he would lay on a run.

The bus had to be started by means of a huge handle pushed into a hole below the bonnet. This had to be swung while someone adjusted the throttle lever on the steering column. It usually took several efforts before the engine sprang into life, but once started she went with a bang – often literally, since there were always frequent backfires from the exhaust. There was a handbrake on the outside of the chassis which sometimes had to be used to hold her back going down our steeper hills. I do not know what make the bus was, but I think it may well have been one of the original Bedfords. Travelling in her provided a very bumpy ride; could the tyres have been solid? It certainly felt like it.

Passengers were accommodated in four rows of seats across the bus, into which you had to clamber by way of a running board which graced one side. It was usually open to the four winds in spite of having a collapsible canvas roof which could be pulled up over the passengers in very bad weather. This Mr Knight was always reluctant to do, since it frequently got stuck half-way up, resulting in consequent delay to the journey.

We seldom had the thrill of a ride in Knight's bus because Father had a car, so we usually went with him in that to the station or into Plymouth, but I do remember once the thrill of going to Liskeard in the bus.

This was one of Mr Knight's specials. He never had a regular schedule, but from time to time would put up a notice in the village shop to announce a destination, and anyone wishing to go with him put their name down on the list. The time of departure was at the bottom. If you lived beyond the Post Office you joined the bus at the time of leaving, while others who lived along the route would be picked up on the way.

On this particular morning, my sister and I were at our gate well in advance of the advertised time of departure. Mother, who was going with us, remained in the house. We were to run in and fetch her as soon as we heard the bus coming. This was not difficult, as long before it rounded the bend we could hear the hideous klaxon horn which announced its passage. We rushed in to fetch Mother as it pulled up outside. Immense excitement as we clambered up the steep step and settled ourselves on the hard seats.

Some of the passengers were already on board. Mrs Toms, a farmer's fat wife, was wedged between the two Pengelly sisters.

'Be you going to the shops, me dear?' she asked Mother.

When she was told the main purpose of our trip was to get our hair cut, she expressed some disapproval of such extravagance.

'Why, I allus cuts our Janet's hair meself – but then your girls have got such lovely curls, haven't they?'

I squirmed in my seat at the thought of my curls, and wished I had Janet's straight pudding basin hair-cut. I was never allowed to have mine cut short, but never mind; today we were going to town. We might even go to the book-shop and be able to spend our pocket money on the greatest treasure, a book. If this was followed by lunch at The Bull, it would be a red letter day indeed.

We drove through the village, picking up other passengers as we went. Then down the steep hill into Seaton, the next hamlet, where we collected up two baskets of eggs and a crate of noisy ducklings. Through the Hessenford valley, deeply wooded on both sides, with the clear river running down its bottom to the sea. It was Easter time, and the banks and woods were studded with primroses, growing thick as clotted cream under the trees and hedges.

Mr Knight was not a good driver. He always went as fast as his ancient vehicle could be pushed, but there was so little traffic on the roads in those days, none of the farms had mechanised equipment, so all one was likely to meet was a lumbering farm cart or a farmer in his trap.

Careering along in the bus was an exciting ride for us children. With a plume of blue smoke billowing out behind, and the wind rushing past our ears, it was easy to enjoy fantasies of being in Boadicea's chariot, or galloping with Robin Hood through Sherwood Forest.

We pulled up in the market square in Liskeard, and alighted with some difficulty from the high seats. Everyone gathered up their baskets, and, with admonitions from our driver not to be late for the return trip, we set off to our various destinations.

Mr Knight never waited for anyone and always left for the homeward journey at four o'clock. It was rumoured that on occasions he had left people behind even if they had paid their return fares.

I suppose that particular day was no different from others when we went into town, but I remember it for two things. I was allowed to have my ringlets cut short, and we went to the bookshop where I bought a copy of *King Solomon's Mines*, which opened up the wonderful world of Rider Haggard to me.

You may wonder what happened to the bus. Well, it had an unfortunate end. Some years after we travelled in it for the last time, Mr Knight was returning home alone one night and simply ran off the road into a deep ditch. He was not hurt and no one suggested that he was inebriated at the time. Apparently he got out and left the wreck where it lay. I can remember seeing it, a rusty heap beside the road, years later when I went back to the village. It may be there still for all I know, though I fear it is much more likely to be buried under a swathe of concrete which probably cuts brutally through the winding Cornish lanes.

6. The Great Western Railway

THE G.W.R. I don't know when I first asked my Father what those letters stood for, but I know how splendid I thought the railway was from the first time I travelled on it. Curiously enough I cannot remember arriving at Paddington Station, only the thrill of entering the great smokey cavern which was where the train which would take us to Cornwall would be standing. Whenever we had been visiting our Grandmother in St Albans this was the train which would take us home!

We would arrive in a taxi at platform one. A porter piled our luggage on to a barrow, and led the way to our compartment. Grasping our own belongings, which in my case usually includes some sort of livestock, white mice in a cage; goldfish in a jar and probably a dog on a lead, we went through the great circular booking office on to platform one, where the train would be waiting. The engine puffed away quietly at the end, the plateman walked along the carriages tapping the wheels with his long hammer. High above on the wall was the great two-faced clock and beneath it the Tommy, arms outstretched beneath his cape, who commemorated the men who had so recently fallen in the Great War.

Once at the compartment, the luggage would be put on racks and under the seats. The third class compartments in those days had seats each side and a sliding door into the corridor which ran the length of the train. As we were usually a party of six or seven we usually reserved one for the journey. As there were only two window seats there was usually an argument as to who should have them. This was settled by Mother, who divided the journey between us, and I seem to remember we always had to change into a window seat when the train reached Dawlish, which I suppose was about half way between London and our destination.

The G.W.R. seat cushions were covered in chocolate brown material, which with yellow and gold were the colours of the line. All the railways had their own colours, and we thought ours was by the far the best, feeling the green of the Southern to be much inferior. At the back of each seat was a little linen antimacassar for adults to rest their heads on, above these were photos of beauty spots along the line. We were very pleased when these were places in Cornwall, but sometimes they were in other counties with names which puzzled me. Bath and Wells was one. It did not show either a bath or a well!

We loved the pictures of Plymouth Hoe because we knew it well, and Dawlish Warren was another favourite suggesting as it did dozens of rabbits coming out of their burrows to see us rush by.

Having settled the seating arrangements, if we were in good time, Father would take us along to look at the engine, and perhaps speak to the driver. What splendid monsters the engines were. Painted bright green, with their names in gold letters on a curved plaque. Splendid names too, the *Windsor Castle*, *George the Fourth* or the *Duke of York*. If we were lucky the engine driver would talk to us and show us the cord he would pull to whistle us away at the start of our journey.

When the time for departure came we walked back to our compartment past the guard's van with its jumble of luggage, bicycles and parcels; the mail van filled with the canvas sacks of letters some of which would be flung out at wayside stations as the train flew past. Then we passed the first class carriages next to the dining car with silk shades on the table lamps and shining silver, back to our place on the train.

When the exact time for departure came we were allowed to lean out of the window and watch as the guard signalled to the driver. The guard stood on the platform, a large pocket watch in one hand, his green flag folded in the other. At the exact moment he put the watch back in his waistcoat pocket, he unfurled the flag, took his whistle from the end of its silver chain and blew.

As the flag waved above his head there was a blast from the engine. The great train seemed to take a huge breath and began to move. As the door to the guard's van slid past him he swung himself expertly in to the train. Slowly the platform changed, past people waving, past fish crates waiting to be loaded on to the night train down to Plymouth for the morning's catch. We ran out of the gloom of the station into the daylight. We were on our way.

Sometimes there was the thrill of being seen off by the Station Master himself. If an important person was known to be travelling this splendid person appeared from his office wearing a tail coat and shiny top hat. Crowds melted before him, the 'important person' (whoever it might be), would be seen to be comfortably installed, the top hat which had been doffed would be put back on the Station Master's head and he stalked back to his office.

The first part of the journey tended to be a little dull. Sliding past the backs of houses in Royal Oak and Ealing, through stations with names like music hall turns, Hayes and Harlington; West Drayton and Yiewsley; on to Slough where we looked out for the big sign of the cup of the bedtime beverage. It began to be more interesting when we went over the bridge at Maidenhead, with tiny boats and punts rocking on the river below. Then Reading, with its two very important products, Huntley and Palmers biscuits and Sutton's Seeds. At this point, perhaps it was the thought of the biscuits, we began to feel hungry, and we asked if perhaps we could have lunch. Sometimes this was agreed to, sometimes we had to wait until we flashed past some place like Swindon. We always had a picnic lunch on the journey. Mother had packed a basket of sandwiches, fruit biscuits and chocolate, with thermos of tea for the adults and lemonade for children. We spread napkins over our laps and munched away happily as the countryside flashed past the windows.

We did not usually eat in the dining car, though on one very special occasion, when I was travelling with an Uncle he gave me tea on the train, a very special treat. It was exciting walking down the swaying train, over the wobbly concertina couplings where, between the coaches, you could see the gravel track through gaps in the floor. It seemed to be rushing backwards. Then into the dining car to be offered a splendid tea. This started with toasted tea cakes, followed by a selection of sandwiches, and finally slices of fruit or Madeira cake. How much I admired the skill with which the waiter managed to pour tea into cups as he swayed with the motion of the train, never spilling a drop.

As we swept along we looked out for favourite towns and villages. We recognised advertisements which stood in the fields beside the track.

No great billboards in those days, usually cut out figures. Carter's Little Liver Pills was a joke because of our surname. We used to ask Father if they were anything to do with him, and he answered rather ruefully he wished they were, he would be a lot richer if he sold pills rather than the wine which was his business. Other signs which I remember very well were the two painters carrying their plank shoulder high who represented Hall's Paints, and the sturdy bull calf boasting about the strength of Bovril.

Lunch over, we settled down to read until the train slowed down to begin the run through Exeter. The Cornishman made a non-stop run to Plymouth but it slowed a little as it got to Devon which we recognised by the rich red soil and the stocky red cattle grazing in the fields.

The first sight of the sea was at Dawlish, and the excitement of running along a track so close to the water that it seemed we must plunge over the edge into the muddy estuary, where sea birds and waders did not seem at all alarmed by the train tearing past them.

Soon we asked how long it would be before we got to Plymouth, and the inevitable reply, not long now. We were allowed to get out and stretch our legs at North Road Station as the train always stopped there for a few minutes before going on into Cornwall.

If there was time we were able to go to the bookstall and spend any money left over from the holiday. I always bought my favourite weekly, the Rover. This boy's paper was wonderful, with its adventure serials which took place in far flung corners of the Empire, so exciting one could hardly wait from one week to another for the story to unfold.

Back in the carriage the train moved off on the last stage of the journey. We wiped off some of the grime collected on the trip with rather grubby handkerchiefs, put on our gloves and hats to be ready to get out at our tiny station.

The train was now running through the industrial areas of the great port with the dockyard area where the funnels and masts of many ships could be seen through gaps in the streets of tiny houses. Suddenly there was the thrill of seeing Saltash Bridge. No matter how many times one goes over that miracle of engineering it never fails to astound by its originality and beauty. We watched as the engine curved round ahead of us, and down below was the Tamar, with the busy traffic of ships and chain-drawn ferry passing in mid-stream. We slid through Saltash Station and on to St Germans – our stop, where the train only stopped if there were passengers on board who had made prior arrangements to get out there. We jumped out, and watched the train disappear round the corner on its way to Penzance. We were home!

7. Special Friends

MY first 'grown-up friends of my very own', as I liked to call them, were two elderly spinster ladies who lived in our little Cornish village.

I was a rather solitary child, being the middle girl of a very spaced-out family; my elder sister was away at boarding school, and the younger one was too young to join in my many outdoor activities. This did not, however, prevent me from having a very happy time pursuing my own interests in what seemed to me to be an entirely satisfactory way.

One thing I liked particularly was going to Church. Not, it must be admitted, because of any deep religious beliefs, but for the music. My parents were not regular attenders at our services, so I often went alone, and this is how I first met my special friends.

The elder of the two, Miss Minna, played the organ when she was at home. She was a very good organist and, being a passionate lover of music, she tried to carry our rather staid congregation beyond the limits of four line hymns. We tackled many unusual settings to our psalms and Te Deums when she was in charge, and even tried the odd anthem for special occasions. It was her playing which introduced me to classical music.

At home my experience lay between Father's liking for the *Dead March* in *Saul*, or *In a Monastery Garden*, while Mother did not get beyond the latest musical comedy melodies.

One evening after the service I found myself walking beside Minna, and something prompted me to tell her how much I enjoyed her playing. The result was an invitation to her house to listen to some of her records, and thus began a friendship which was one of the treasures of my childhood.

Special Friends

Although at first my Mother was uncertain of the propriety of accepting an invitation from someone 'we didn't know', that is to say to whom she had not been properly introduced, luckily for me my new friend appreciated the niceties of our narrow social life. She left her card to endorse the invitation, thus clearing the way for my visit to be approved.

Although later knowledge of her ideas made it quite clear she had no time for such tiresome conventions, and I am sure would have hailed a peasant in the Algarve or an Arab in the desert as her equals, in my case her acceptance of custom enabled me to set off on the appointed day, wearing my second best dress, and carrying a basket of peaches from our greenhouse as a gift.

The two ladies lived in a bungalow perched high up on the Cornish cliff. It was surrounded by great hedges of fuschia, with a garden path bordered with pink sea thrift, and had a wide verandah covered with roses. The unusual name 'Eudora' was painted on the gate. I never discovered the origin of that name, but the gate on which it was painted opened up a whole new world to me. I have often wondered since whether the present owners have retained the name. I hope so. I would not like to think it had become 'Chez Nous' or 'Bide-a-While'!

When I knocked on the door for the first time, I was met, not by Miss Minna, but another lady whom I recognised as her companion. A round, twinkling little person, who ushered me in with a smile, saying, 'You must be our new friend; come in and we'll make the tea.'

This was the sort of welcome calculated to put any shy ten-year-old at ease, and from that moment I was completely at home in the house.

After having been regaled with a sumptuous tea of scones with Cornish cream and home-made strawberry jam, followed by saffron cake that melted in the mouth, my gift of peaches was graciously accepted and the real treat began.

'Now,' said Minna, 'we'll have some music.'

She went to a cabinet in the corner of the room and took out a record. A moment later the soaring notes of *Jesu, Joy of Man's Desiring* filled the room. I sat entranced, and when it was finished none of us spoke for a few moments. Then, feeling some comment was called for, I blurted out, 'That was wonderful – just like the sea in the early morning.'

I don't know why I remember the scene so vividly, even the very words I used, but it is as clear today as it was on that summer day over sixty years ago. Long after, when I heard Myra Hess play the same music at one of the lunch-time concerts in the National Gallery during the Blitz, I was immediately carried back to that little sitting room, with its crowds of books and pictures, and the scent of roses from a jug on the table.

My new friends were a remarkable couple. They belonged to that group of indomitable Victorian women who journeyed all over the world, recording their trips in carefully kept diaries and letters. Some of these writings they published, illustrated with sketches of remarkably high quality. They had exotic names like *An English Lady's Travels in Tunisia*, or *Teneriffe, and Her Six Satellites*. Very good reading there is in them, and if you can find a copy in the stacks of a library, or among the battered volumes of a second-hand dealer's tray you would do well to purchase it. The minutiae of daily life is so well described, the sights and smells of the places so vividly recalled, they present a better picture than many modern travel writers achieve.

Minna and her friend Bea had known each other since their student days, and had lived together for over fifty years when I first met them. Theirs was one of the most rewarding friendships I have ever known. They had both travelled all over the world, but when I knew them Bea had almost given up travel; it was Minna who still went away on trips. She was perhaps the more intellectual one, Bea was artistic and domesticated, so my memories of visits to 'Eudora' are mostly of Bea. With her I spent many hours sitting in front of the fire or on the verandah, reading the long letters which came from the far-away places Minna was visiting. If it was a place Bea knew, she would describe it in wonderful detail, or if it was a place she had not been to, we would look it up in the *Encyclopaedia Britannica* or other reference books and form our own ideas about the country.

My friends presented somewhat unusual appearances on their outings into the village. In summer they wore tailored suits of linen or shantung, with skirts to mid-calf; on their feet, sandals, and their headgear was either an old tropical sun-helmet lined with green, or on Sundays raffia hats suitably adorned with flowers. In winter the suits were of a long-jacketed style, made of tweed they wove themselves. If it looked like rain they wore immense mackintosh capes. Headgear was either a tweed bonnet to match the suit, or a wide brimmed felt hat. They carried stout ash walking sticks, green sunshades or black umbrellas, and always voluminous string bags from which they produced an astonishing variety of fascinating objects. At home they wore smocks with large pockets into which they put the implements or tools of whatever activity they happened to be engaged in at the time. Since their hobbies were numerous, ranging from gardening to fern pressing, bookbinding, painting, and etching, they used a wide range of items.

The only time I saw them dressed up, so to speak, was Christmas. As my friendship with them grew, to my great joy my parents asked them to join us for dinner. Then they appeared in black silk or velvet dresses of late Edwardian style, with velvet ribbons round their necks, and fine cameo brooches pinned decorously on lace collars.

Minna was a real 'blue-stocking'. She had earned a degree in comparative religion before degrees were awarded to women. Both she and Bea had studied philosophy at university, and were excellent linguists. They spoke French, German and Italian fluently. Minna also spoke Swedish as she had many friends in Sweden and visited that country nearly every year.

One result of this last talent was a rather disastrous meeting of the Mothers' Union. My Mother, being President at the time, and hard pressed for a speaker for the monthly gathering, and having heard me boast about by friend's skills, suggested she might give a talk to the members. She chose as her topic *Legends of Sweden*. It was to be illustrated with slides which it was my unhappy duty to flash onto a sheet hung at the back of the village hall. It was never likely to capture the interest of our local women. I suffered an uneasy hour during her lecture, the end of which was greet with evident relief before a concerted rush to the tea tables. By dint of some discreet eavesdropping among the tea cups I was able to catch remarks like, 'They furriners be a queer lot, I fancy,' and 'I don't rightly like the look of their goings on, do 'ee my dear?'

I often wonder why some parents fail to realise the importance to a child of friends outside the family circle. Such friendships are very special and they should be respected. They are the beginnings of independent ideas and opinions, some of which may not be totally acceptable but are nevertheless valuable. I am very grateful that I was encouraged in my special friendships which meant so much to me. To friends outside the family circle one was able to disclose criticisms of family without a sense of disloyalty. Moral and religious doubts were talked over dispassionately. Subjects I did not discuss at home provided many long talks with Minna and Bea. Foreigners, politics, religion, even sex in a guarded way, were all grist to our conversational mill. Nothing was ever treated with bigotry or intolerance.

As the years passed, Minna continued to go off on her travels and Bea and I shared her long letters. Often we would select what we felt to be appropriate music in response to her news. We had Delius when she wrote from France, Grieg or Sibelius when the letters were from Sweden, and Wagner thundered through the little house when she was in Germany.

When I was fifteen we moved away from the village, and from then on my only contact was through letters and the presents they sent me for Christmas and birthdays. I still have some of them: a tiny Swedish knife in a leather case; Swiss book-ends with eidleweiss painted on the ends; and a prayer book, beautifully inscribed by Bea, 'To my friend Anne, on the occasion of her Confirmation, June 1934.'

In 1937, Minna died while on a visit to Sweden. I tried to write a letter to Bea which would express what their friendship had meant to me. I hope my clumsy effort told her what I really felt.

It was not until 1941, when on leave from the Air Force, I was able to visit Bea again. I was delighted to find that, in spite of failing eyesight, she was still managing to live in the bungalow overlooking the Atlantic.

How thrilled she was to see me! What admiration for my uniform, and interest in my work. She was relieved to hear I did not have to fight, though I am sure she would have been quite prepared to do so had the enemy ever arrived at the gate of 'Eudora'.

When I said goodbye to her, she did something she had never done before. She reached up and kissed me gently on both cheeks, saying wistfully, 'How well Minna would have looked in that uniform.'

I did not see her again. In 1943 she suffered a stroke and was taken to the local hospital. In 1944 I saw in *The Times* that she had died, as it said, 'peacefully, at the age of 88'. So my dear special friends went out of my life. I like to think of them in some comfortable Heaven, arguing gently the respective merits of Brahms and Beethoven as musicians, and whether Scott was a greater novelist than Hardy.

I don't know which way the argument would have gone, but I am for ever grateful to them for having started *me* on the critical path.

8. Old Tom

I MUST have been about nine when I first went out with Tom. One morning I woke up very early, and when I moved, Susan, Father's labrador, who always slept between my sister's and my bed, got up and poked her nose into my hand. Her tail waved gently, but I had to tell her, 'Not this morning, girl. I'm going fishing with Tom. Lie down, you can't come.'

It was still quite cold and she was not reluctant to return to her rug. I slipped out of bed and put on a thick sweater and shorts, and picked up a pair of sandshoes. I knew the rest of the household would not be stirring for at least another hour, and I felt quite proud of managing to wake so early. I went to the kitchen and slipped out of the back door, closing it quietly behind me.

I ran across the garden, and down the cliff path which led down to the beach. The sun was coming up over the bay, but a thick haze still lay over the water. It made the waves look like the opals in my Mother's rings.

Thinking of Mother reminded me that I was not supposed to run about barefoot. I ought to be wearing my shoes, but I didn't mind that she thought that I was too much of a Tomboy. Father laughed at that, and said there would be plenty of time to grow into a young lady. I loved being barefoot, to feel the ground under my toes. There were so many different feelings. I thought of them as I ran down to the shore. Sand, smooth and scrunchy; mud, soft and squelchy; grass, soft as a cushion; and rocks, warm and solid, when you caught your breath as you jumped from one to another over the rock pools.

I was very excited that morning. I was going to meet Old Tom.

Tom was a local fisherman, an old hand respected in the village. When I had first met him I had only ventured a shy 'Good morning' as I went past along the beach, but the old man began to acknowledge my greeting, and one day he invited me to sit beside him as he worked on his nets. His gnarled hands made wonderfully dextrous movements as he mended the holes, or twisted the wicker to make the round lobster pots. They had inverted curved entrances, and sat on the sea bed inviting any unwary lobster passing by to walk in.

I asked Tom about his pots, and why some people used the flat ones, and he replied, '*They* bain't no good. You'll lose more lobsters from them things than you'll catch. T'would take a cunning ole lobster to get out of one of *my* pots.'

Our friendship had matured slowly, but soon there were very few days during the holidays which did not find me sitting beside the old man, listening to his stories, and now and again asking questions. I soon found out that if I did not ask too many questions, he would tell me all sorts of interesting things about fishing and sea birds and all the other creatures of the seashore.

Once in a while he would talk about himself. He had lived all his life in the village, and seemed to be related to everyone in the place. He was reputed to be over eighty.

'Stands ter reason he must be all of that,' the broad Cornish voices would argue as they stood round their boats at the foot of the slipway. 'He were in that old Boer War, that I do know. Got a couple of medals to prove it, too.'

I had never seen the medals, but as Tom was my idol, I was sure that he must have been a fine soldier, and deserved all the medals he may have been given.

One day, after we had finished a long discussion about the habits of mackerel, I plucked up my courage and asked him if I might go out with him to help him pull up his pots.

'Well,' he had replied slowly, 'I don't rightly know about that. A nice young lady like you. What would you be wanting with a rough ole job lifting pots?'

'Oh, Tom, I'd really love to come. I could help with the boat and everything. I wouldn't get in the way, I promise.'

'Well, you must ask your Father first. If he says it's alright, I might take you along one morning.'

To my surprise and joy, when I told my Father this he agreed at once. 'Alright, you can swim quite well now, and he's a decent old chap. Do what he tells you, and bring us back a lobster!'

As I ran along the beach that morning, I looked anxiously for Tom. Would he be waiting for me? Would he have forgotten that I was to go that day? Was I too late?

As I got near his boat I heaved a sigh of relief, for there was Tom, coming down the path from his cottage, carrying a coil of line over his shoulder, his empty pipe sticking out of the corner of his mouth, and his blue woollen cap perched on the back of his head.

'So you got up early then, did yer?' was his greeting. 'I thought you'd be lying abed!'

'Of course not, you said I could come today, so here I am. It's a good morning, isn't it?'

'Arh, it be fair enough I reckon, but you'll have to work a bit. We'll pull out to pick up the pots, then maybe on the way back we'll put out a line for mackerel.'

I was in seventh heaven! To be going potting and then trawl for mackerel was more than I had dared to hope for.

I tied the laces of my shoes together and put them round my neck. Old Tom put a roller under the boat, and together we pushed it. It ran surprisingly easy over the shingle to the water's edge. He threw the lines aboard, and I jumped in to push off with an oar as he gave a final shove into the sea.

The little boat rocked gently as we settled ourselves for the trip out into the bay, to the spot where the old man's pots were anchored. I sat in the stern and handled the tiller as well as I was able. It was not really necessary for me to steer, but I like the feeling of importance it gave me as I watched Tom take long pulls on his oars.

By now the sun had broken through, and the slight swell was increasing as the tide turned and began to run out. As we moved from the shore I watched the cormorants diving from the top of the big rock the locals called the Shag. The elongated figures of the birds stood like statues on top of the pile, and then dropped like stones into the sea below. As they did so, gulls rose in a screaming flock from the surface of the water where they had been riding gently up and down on the swell. Then up came the cormorants far out in the waves,, and flopped clumsily back onto their perch on the rock.

As we approached the place where his pots were, Tom beckoned to me to come and take the oars while he got ready to haul up. I had learned to row the previous summer, so I scrambled to his seat and took the oars. It was a struggle to manage them. They were old and heavy, but I held on as well as I could to keep the boat straight. Tom reached over to grab the first float, and shouted, 'That'll do then; heave to.'

I shipped the oars with a sigh of relief, and rested them on the gunwales as he pulled up the first pot. Slowly it appeared over the side of the boat, but it was empty so he threw it back, and it slid down into the sea and disappeared from sight. The next pot had two large lobsters crawling about in the bottom. I hoped that Tom would not ask me to take them out, they looked enormous and very angry. I was very relieved when he got hold of them by the back and quickly dropped them into the crate which lay on the bottom of the boat.

'I reckon they be a bit nippy for you, me dear,' he said. 'You watch the line when I throw her over, don't let 'er snag as she goes.'

We spent the next hour moving down the line of pots and emptying those that had anything in them. Soon there was a pile of lobsters in the crate, and a couple of good size crabs keeping them company.

When Tom came to the end of his pots, he said we would be going back; and, taking a line from his locker, he told me to sit in the stern and try a trawl for mackerel. He took the oars and, turning towards shore, began to pull towards home. The lines were baited with silver spinners which shone and quivered as the force of the water pulled them. As we moved shorewards, a gust of wind blew up suddenly. I looked towards the horizon and saw heavy black clouds had appeared out to sea. The boat rocked heavily as the swell increased, and there were white horses running towards us from the west.

For a moment, my interest in what might be on my line was distracted. What if we couldn't make it back? What if the boat capsized? I had heard that Tom could not swim; it was the fishermen's superstition that it was better not to swim if you met disaster at sea, drown quickly seemed to be their philosophy. I was very frightened, and asked Tom nervously,

'Shall we get back alright?'

'Of course we will, me dear, I'll just pull down shore a bit, we may have to pull in along Low's Cove, but don't you worry, this will soon blow over. You just mind your line, haven't you got a bite yet?'

I dragged in the line and saw we had a couple of decent sized mackerel on it. I was quite proud that my lessons the previous summer had hardened me to the task of taking them off the hooks, and I managed to dislodge them quickly and neatly.

Tom obviously approved, for he said, 'We'll make a fisherman of you yet, and what will your Mother think of that then?'

I preferred not to think of Mother's reaction to this activity, and went about throwing the line back into the sea.

We were now rocking pretty heavily, but what with minding my fishing, and trying to hang onto the tiller, I didn't have much time to worry. A half hour later we made land, and pulled up in a cove a half mile away from our village.

'Reckon if we just stay here a while she'll blow over, and then we can get back. You hungry?' Tom asked.

Suddenly I felt famished, and said so.

'Well, why don't we cook one of those mackerel you caught? You find a bit of driftwood, and we'll soon get him cooked.'

Once we had lit the wood and let it burn down to red embers, Tom cleaned and slit open a fish and held it expertly on a stick over the coals. He produced an old enamel plate from his locker, and divided the fish between us. I cannot remember a meal which tasted as delicious as that I shared with Tom on the Cornish beach nearly seventy years ago.

When we had finished and I had wiped my fingers on the seat of my shorts in imitation of Tom's use of his trousers, we covered the fire with sand, and set off for home. The squall had died as quickly as it had started, and we soon ran up onto our own beach.

Tom chose one of the lobsters from the crate and gave it to me, saying, 'You give this to your Father with my compliments, and say I was glad to have you along as my mate.'

As I walked home, dangling my lobster from the piece of string which I had tied round its tail, I doubt if there was a happier child in the West Country.

9. The Visitors

EVERY Summer from mid-July to September, the village played host to the visitors. Not day trippers or foreign tourists in those days, but families who came to spend the school holidays by the sea.

There were no hotels or boarding houses in our area, so some came to stay in houses they owned and kept for holiday use, but the majority rented rooms from the village people who gave over their bedrooms and parlours to lodgers. The farmers and cottagers often put their families out to sleep in barns or tents. The wives catered, providing all meals, and very good food it was – fresh fish and shellfish from the locals, home-grown vegetables from their gardens and clotted cream in abundance. The money they made from the visitors supplied a considerable part of many families' income. Early in July there was a buzz of information and gossip round the village, and we began to pester the locals to find out who had booked rooms and where.

'I hear the Maxwells are going to Mrs Thomas again then – their boys will have grown a bit, I dare say.'

'The Brodies are going to Henley's Farm again. There's a new baby and they are bringing a Nanny. *That* won't suit Mrs Henley if she gets into her kitchen!'

Everyone did well out of the visitors. Particularly Mr Greet who ran the only taxi service. He was always fully booked fetching people from St Germans, our local station, where the Cornishman stopped on its way from Paddington to Penzance.

Mr Greet's car was a large old American Packard with a huge trunk fine for carrying all the luggage and holiday paraphernalia brought for

51

seaside activities. Prawning nets, buckets and spades, cricket bats and golf clubs all loaded into Greet's taxi with the luggage.

Most of the visiting children were from Service families whose fathers were serving in India or Egypt or some other part of the Empire. During the term they went to boarding schools and in holidays were with grandparents or aunts when their parents were not on leave.

I had one particular friend, Philippa, whose arrival I looked forward to with happy anticipation. Her father was in the Army, serving in Egypt in the Camel Corps, which sounded tremendously romantic to me. She had a younger sister, Jean, the same age as my sister Maureen, so we made a good quartet. I have to admit we tried to shake off the young ones as often as we could, pursuing activities too difficult for them to cope with. They came with their grandmother, who took rooms near our house every year, and I think was relieved, after getting to know my parents, to know they were safe in our house and garden.

The grandmother was a rather formidable old lady – Grannies in those days could be quite frightening. They seemed very old, unlike the grans of today. Our Granny was not at all frightening, and although she always wore black or mauve, because she was a widow, and a hat until lunchtime, she was not at all forbidding. I think she probably spoiled us by the standards of those days, and we loved her dearly.

Philippa was a tomboy like me, and we got up to all sorts of exciting projects in the garden and on the beach.

One year we built a tree-house in a pine tree on the cliff – a considerable effort which entailed much begging, borrowing and pilfering materials and tools from the adults. I still have a scar on my thumb caused by over-zealous use of a sharp chisel when building that tree-house. I did have some tools of my own, as carpentry was one of my hobbies, but for such a large project we needed to borrow some of my Father's, and he was always very reluctant to lend his tools. However, we finally managed to build a structure into which we climbed by way of a rope ladder. This could be drawn up out of sight, and gave us a vantage point to watch people on the path below and drop pine-cones onto unsuspecting heads.

We also managed to purloin an old telescope which we used to scan the horizon and watch passing ships.

We used to take 'provisions' cadged from cook or save surreptitiously from meals up into our refuge and drank lemonade or ginger pop out of the bottle, while we were pirates or explorers depending on which books we were reading at the time. Kipling, Stevenson and Scott were all favourites. Sometimes we read Angela Brazil's schoolgirl stories. These we raced through and secretly admitted we thought they were 'soppy'. We spent hours on the beach, paddling in the rock pools when the tide was out, swimming when the breakers came up the shore.

We collected illustrated books like the *Observer* series, which helped us to identify the different creatures whose brilliant colours made such wonderful moving pictures below the water as it ebbed and flowed with the tide.

We made 'collections' of seaweed and hung the strands round the walls of the bathing hut, carefully labelling our specimens, and were always surprised and disappointed to see their shapes and colours disappear as they dried out away from the sea.

On wet days we 'camped out' in the hut or under makeshift bits of canvas and mackintosh stretched over the rocks on the shore. We cooked meals on a battered primus stove and were shipwrecked sailors or Indians hiding from the Redcoats.

When the weather was good we built driftwood fires on the beach and baked potatoes in the embers. No potato ever tasted as good as those blackened ones we pulled from the camp fire and slit open with our penknives.

I had cousins who visited us during the Summer but they were all boys and older than me, so when I was allowed to join in their games it was always as a girl – a 'helper'. I never queried this male superiority, and was duly grateful when I was given the job of fetching buckets of water to fill the moat of a particularly elaborate sandcastle, or always having to field on the boundary during cricket matches.

Girls were not supposed to understand the value and importance of cigarette cards, but I remember being very superior one year when I produced a complete set of 'Player's' cricketers which my cousin Ken could only match with an incomplete set of racing drivers.

Most of the visitors mixed with each other and the locals in the village activities, but there was one family who caused much gossip.

An attractive young woman with four little boys ranging in age between five and nine arrived one Summer and rented a house on the outskirts of the village which belonged to a lawyer from Launceston. Renting a house was unusual in itself, as most visitors came to their own or lodged with the locals. The boys were looked after by a young man who looked like an undergraduate and was obviously acting as a holiday tutor.

Speculation was rife as to who they were. Where did they come from, and was it proper for her to be in the house with the young man? Surely the children should have a nanny or at least a governess? Some of the gossip filtered down to us children in spite of the fact that conversations always ended abruptly when adults saw we were listening. However, by dint of pretending to be absorbed in the choice of sweets or a spade in the village shop one overheard such comments as, 'No one know where they come from. Mrs Pengelly heard London – but no letters come from there for 'er.' (All letters were scrutinised in the Post Office before Jim took them out on his rounds).

The village woman who was engaged to 'do' for them could provide no better information, though she did say, 'She's a good payer – don't mind a bit extra on the bill.'

The boys were not encouraged to join in our games on the beach, but stayed with their male guardian, who did seem to be resourceful in keeping them amused. The boys were always dressed in identical grey flannel shorts and shirts, brown sandals and if the sun was hot, floppy white hats.

They did not appear in Church on Sundays as most visitors did – another source of adverse comment from the locals.

One day when Philipa and I were prawning in pools near to where the family were sitting, we dared each other to go and speak to the boys. We worked our way closer, pool by pool, until we confronted the two older boys across the rocks. Their mother and the young man were sitting some way up the beach and out of earshot, so I ventured a nervous,

'Hello, any luck?'

'Yes, we've got some big ones; want to see them?' one of the boys replied.

We all squatted down to examine their catch, a number of prawns scrabbling about in the bottom of a bucket.

'Those *are* good,' said Philippa admiringly, 'Will you have them for tea?'

'I expect so,' was the reply. 'I love them, but Tom, that's the baby, won't eat them.'

Emboldened by this exchange, we asked, 'What are your names? I'm Anne and this is my friend, Philippa. I live here, but she only comes in the holidays.'

'You *are* lucky – you mean you live here all the year round? I wish *we* did. I'm John and this is Peter, my twin. David and Tom are the babies. I'm the eldest.'

'Yes, but only by two hours,' said Peter.

'We've often seen you on the beach,' I said. 'Would you like to come and see our collections? They're in the hut over there.'

'We'll have to ask Matthew – he's our tutor for the Summer,' John replied, and set off up the beach to ask permission.

I could see from the adults' attitude that permission was not being granted. The young man came down the beach to where we were waiting and said,

'I'm afraid the boys have to go home now,' and turned away, followed by the boys' protestations.

'I bet it's because we're girls,' said Philippa angrily. 'Anyway, I don't care – we know much better prawning places than they do,' and we ran back down to the rock pools.

As far as I can remember, we never tried to approach the 'grey boys', as we called them, again. The mystery about their background was never solved.

10. Carnival and Flower Show

CARNIVAL was the highlight of the summer holidays.

For weeks before the event, which always took place on August Bank holiday, plans were being laid by the contestants. Which section should they enter, what characters would they represent, and most important of all how they would keep their plans secret.

There were several classes. Mounted which meant on horseback, then vehicle which could be horsedrawn or mechanical, then other wheeled items such as bicycles, prams, barrows or handcarts. Last of all the humble pedestrians, anyone who got into fancy dress and joined the procession on foot.

The village shop laid in extra stocks of crêpe paper, ribbons and balloons in anticipation of the demand, and some people even made trips to the local town for materials. Plans were kept secret, though some dubious methods had been known to be used to wheedle out information regarding rivals' plans.

We children usually had to compete in the pedestrian or bicycle classes but one year a cousin of mine and I got together with a group of our visitor friends and decided to get into the vehicle class. But how? There was no way Father would let us have the car, and anyway our dear chauffeur Price would never have consented to drive us. Mr Greet's taxi had been commandeered by the family lodging at his house. The farm trucks had all been spoken for, when suddenly some-one had the idea of Mitchell's truck. This was the half ton lorry which he used for general haulage round the village including the weekly rubbish collection. One of our group came from the family which had rooms at the Mitchell's so was well placed to make the initial approach. We awaited the reply with some anxiety.

We had decided we would turn the truck into a pirates' cave.

Materials for this lay all to hand. Sand, rocks and seaweed from the beach. Our costumes would be pyjamas tucked into gum boots. With sashes and cardboard cutlasses, black eye patches, we had in our imagination already won the first prize.

Thomas returned with the devastating news that Mr Mitchell had not agreed to lend us the truck. Dismay all round, but it seemed on certain conditions he might change his mind.

We had to get our parents' consent, we must promise to clean the truck throughly after we had used it, and it would cost us £2 to hire it for the day of the Carnival. If we could meet these conditions he would drive us himself.

We tackled the money problem first. We pooled all our resources and came up with £1-15-6d. Calculating the week's pocket money we could get up to £1-17-6d. That left a shortfall of 2-6d. Someone said they had a birthday that week and could rely upon a tip from their grandfather which would make up the necessary amount.

Cleaning the truck would be no problem, but parents' consent might be a bigger obstacle.

We broke up agreeing we would all tackle them that very evening.

I knew I must choose my moment carefully so I waited until my Father was having his evening drink on the verandah before broaching the subject. I told him about our ideas for a pirates cave, and asked his advice about the costumes. He thought it was a good idea so then I told him about Mitchell's truck.

'Mitchell's truck? That's out of the question, he collects the rubbish in that old thing, you can't ride in that.' He could see from my crest-fallen face how disappointed I was, and my protestations about it being clean for us to use, and the fact that he had promised to drive us himself as long as he did not have to dress up as a pirate, persuaded him to give his agreement.

'Oh, alright then, but don't blame me if you get some horrible disease. I'll have a word with Mitchell tomorrow.'

I was over the moon with excitement and rushed off to find my friends with the good news.

We *did* organise the pirates cave, and rode proudly in the procession uttering suitably blood curdling shouts, but I don't think we won a prize. My young sister won once when she went as a scarecrow in some of Father's clothes with straw coming out of a paper bag mask and a broom handle through the sleeves of her coat to hold her arms up, that was very realistic. Anyway, whatever one's costume on foot or mounted, Carnival was always a great day. I never remember it raining though with our climate surely it must have done so sometimes.

If we woke in the morning to see rain, we probably said, as we always did, 'It'll clear when the tide changes' and it usually did.

Whatever the weather, the parade assembled in an adjacent hamlet where there was a flat field with room to organise the march. Then led by the Liskeard town band, wearing Ruritanian style uniforms lavishly adorned with gold braid, we set off to the strains of *Colonel Bogey* or *The Liberty Bell*. As we wound our way through the village, everyone was at their door or garden gate to see us go by. We basked in the admiring comments.

'Who'd 've thought of going as a parcel! That's a clever idea of Mary's'

'Look at little Bobby, doesn't he look sweet as the Pear's Soap boy?'

Advertisements were always popular,, and I remember the Trelawney boys winning a prize when they went as the Halls Paintmen carrying the name of the company on a plank on their shoulders.

When we arrived at Broad's farmyard, the classes were divided and judging took place. I have no idea who the judges were, but I don't think they were local people, perhaps councillors from town, or even visitors if anyone of sufficient importance was staying at the time. Anyway, rosettes were awarded amid cheers, the procession reformed and marched to the end of the village street and then dispersed. The men went to the pub or to do evening chores, while the women and children had tea in the village hall, laid on by the ladies of the W.I.

Another Carnival Day had come and gone, and summer was slipping away.

The Flower Show was an altogether more serious affair. For one thing, children were not involved, except in one class which usually took the form of a miniature garden made on a plate or tray. The results were rather sad, wilted flowers stuck into soil or sand with a piece of mirror or silver paper representing a pond, with a few sea shells for variety. We were never enthusiastic competitors, although our elders said everyone should enter to show support for the organisers.

The other classes were keenly contested. Everyone, from the owner of the smallest cottage garden to the gentry with their large gardens and greenhouses went in for something. I think the categories were pretty much the same every year, so people knew what to grow to fit a particular class. Rivalry was intense.

It was rumoured from time to time that thefts had been perpetrated from gardens or greenhouses, but I don't remember this ever coming to an actual accusation of cheating.

The Show included classes for home baking, jam preserves and wine, so the women were very much involved. It was held in two large marquees put up in the field by the Village Hall, and in the Hall itself. Flowers and vegetables in the tents and baking etc., in the Hall. By noon everything was set out on the trestle tables and the judges began their work.

While this was going on, anxious competitors repaired to the pub, which did a roaring trade, and the village shop almost ran out of ice cream. Finally, at 2 pm the public were allowed back to view the awards.

The vegetables took pride of place. Huge potatoes, scrubbed and arranged in a pyramid, bearing labels like 'King Edwards, 6-of-a-kind', and onions with names that fascinated me – who was 'Ailsa Craig'? and surely 'Captain Bruce' must win a prize. Enormous marrows, and foot-long runner beans covered the tables. Some bore the coveted red First Prize card, but others only achieved 'Very Highly Commended', an award which seemed to me to be much grander.

Next to the vegetables came the flowers – all the brilliant Autumn colours, dahlias, michaelmas daisies, lilies and sweet peas filled the tent with their various scents. They were in every conceivable container from 3-of-a-kind in single glasses to huge arrangements suitable for the altar steps in Church.

There were many admiring and envious remarks from the onlookers.

'Well, he did well with his dahlias this year.'

'That cactus is a real beauty!'

'Her sweet peas are nice, but I reckon Mary's are a better variety.'

Over everything was the mingled smell of canvas, trampled grass, onions and roses.

At the end of the second tent, the home baking made a mouth-watering display. Huge victoria sponges, apple and blackberry pies with a wedge cut out to show their juicy interiors. Thick scones ready to serve as the basis for a cream tea, and yellow saffron cakes, the centrepiece of every Cornish tea table.

One year there was a slight problem with one of our entries in the flower class. We had a gardener called Billy who had very poor sight – in fact he identified plants almost entirely by touch, but he was a very good gardener. He had several peculiar methods, one of which was to plant his potatoes on the night of a full moon, by moonlight. I have seen him doing this as the full moon came up over the sea, making a glistening path out of the Eddystone light. Well, Billy was very keen that we should win prizes at the Show, and one year he urged my Father to enter our dahlias. The class was for three different varieties, but as the time of the Show approached it seemed we really only had two good enough to exhibit. However, the day before the Show, Billy produced three perfect blooms, and when Father asked where the third had come from, he replied quite cheerfully,

'This be one of the Vicar's. He bain't entering dahlias this year, so he won't miss it!'

Father was horrified, and to Billy's chagrin insisted on withdrawing his entry. However, I do remember winning one year with our peaches. This gave Father great pleasure as they were his pride and joy, and to get them to perfection just at the time of the Show required much hard work.

At the end of the day many of the exhibits were put up for sale, and it did not take long to clear the table. There was always a rush for the baking and it literally went like hot cakes. Late in the evening the tents would be struck, and the tables stacked in the corner of the hall. Nothing remained of the Show except two large rectangles of trampled grass and some discarded prize cards.

The Tennis Tournament took place on the three courts in the village: at the Vicarage, the Brownings' and ours. During the week before the tournament, we were all roped in to work on our court; rolling and mowing to get it up to the best condition. Early on the morning of play,

Billy could be seen trundling a little contraption filled with whitewash up and down the lines which had been marked out with string for him to follow.

Names for the tournament had been entered on a list in the village shop, and a draw was made for partners. I think only doubles were played, and it was run on the knock-out American tournament lines. Only adults took part so I never actually played, but we children were employed as ball-boys, which kept us busy as we often had to go down over the cliff to retrieve wild shots.

My Father was a good player, and always enjoyed entertaining the tennis players while Mother kept a supply of lemonade available on the verandah from which competitors watched while waiting their turn to compete.

Umpires were perched precariously on kitchen step-ladders at the side of the court, and at the end of the day the Vicar used to present the prizes on the Vicarage lawn.

The Cricket Match was the last big event of the Summer. Visitors played the village, and who was legally qualified to play for each team was always a matter of dispute. Both sides tried to rope in good players. The visitors usually had to include some schoolboys, and the villagers found some very hefty local farm lads. The match was played on Henley's pasture, the only flat field in the village. Boundaries were over the cliff on one side and into the cowsheds on the other. There were no helmets in those days, and only the wicket keeper wore gloves, so a googly coming up fast off our rough grass pitch was a fearsom thing to face. Scoring was always done by Mr Webb, the village shoemaker, using the hymn number cards borrowed from the church. I seem to remember honours being pretty evenly divided, wins being registered to both sides from year to year.

At the end of August the visitors began to leave. We said tearful good-byes to our friends, with promises of meeting again next year. Luggage was loaded onto cars or Greet's taxi and they disappeared up the hill to the station.

We settled down to the routine of lessons, evenings indoors instead of on the beach, and mothers began a programme of jam making and pickling. The year turned once again towards winter with its storms and cosy evenings in front of the fire.

11. Plymouth

DURING term time we went into Plymouth once a week.

Looking back on it, I wonder if my Mother was lonely in our new home and way of life. She had lived all her life in a town where her family was well known, and she had a wide circule of friends. Most of them had married and brought up children during the very difficult War years, but before we left to go to live in Cornwall things had begun to get back towards the way they were before the War. Now she was living in a tiny village where there were no social equals except the Vicar and his family, and the rather elderly lady of the manor. I think our trips to town must have been important to her. Although we had visitors during the summer holidays, and she and my Father had become enthusiastic gardeners, I think the trip to see shops and people must have been a link with a different life.

Anyway, we went, usually on a Monday. We made the journey either to the station and then took the train, or, what I liked better, drove all the way and took the ferry to Torpoint. We followed winding lanes, past Tregantle Fort, where my Father's Royal Marine friends were stationed, down through Saltash town to the river Tamar which divided our world, Cornwall, from what the villagers thought of as foreign territory, Devon, England!

As we waited in the queue for the ferry we could see the wide river busy with craft of all kinds. To our right the tall cranes of the dockyard stood up like bony fingers above the grey naval vessels in for repair or refit. Up and down the river all kinds of vessels, tugs, lighters, and patrol boats went about their business in the sort of orderly disorder which seems to work in maritime affairs.

In the middle of the stream the two ferries would be passing as they did every half-hour throughout the day. The one coming our way would grind up onto the shingle beach, the ramp would come down with a crunch as it made contact with the shore.

Following the directions of the crewman, we took our place on the centre deck with all the other vehicles, and with much grinding and clanking the ferry dragged itself to the other shore.

Once in Plymouth, Father took himself off to his office, and Mother and my sisters and I went into town to do the business of the day. This might include a visit to the hairdresser, something which had to be endured, though reluctantly, as he always wanted to let mine grow and curl, while all I wanted was for it to be as short as possible so that I could swim without a cap. Sometimes there was a visit to the dentist, something which I dreaded, particularly if it included having a tooth out. In those days this was done under gas, and I have never forgotten the fight to remain conscious, and the horrible sensation of falling as one succumbed to the anaesthetic.

We usually had some shopping to do, which could be good or bad according to the nature of our purchases. The best for me was the visit to the library. Not the Public Library, of course, for in those days this was thought to be the source of all sorts of infectious diseases. However, Boots the Chemists always had excellent lending libraries in their shops, and the one in Plymouth had a good children's section which was my delight. When I was given my first ticket, and found that the card I received gave me the right to borrow three books from the long shelves, I could hardly believe my luck. To be able to browse among such treasures, and then take them home with me, was wonderful indeed.

What a jumble of authors and subjects I discovered. Ranging from the Angela Brazil school-girl stories, through Henty and Haggard, Dickens and Dumas, my tastes were wide though not very discriminating. But reading was the thing and I could never have enough of it. I can still hear my Mother calling to me to enquire what I was doing, and if my reply was 'Reading', hoping I would not be told to do something more useful.

In the afternoon we went to The Royal Hotel to attend the dancing class. This was held in the ballroom, and was something I heartily disliked. I was a shy child, and dancing came into the category of 'show-ing off', which was a cardinal sin in my code, and although I loved the music which accompanied our clumsy efforts – delicious waltzes and polkas – I did not like standing in rows waving my arms and pointing my toes. Also, one was in constant dread of being singled out to show either how inadequately one performed, or worse still, to be held up as an example of ability. Our teacher was a very formidable lady, Miss Verity, of indeterminate age. She was tall, and always dressed in black, with a white lace collar. She carried a stick with which she beat time, and in moments of stress banged on the floor to show here disapproval of our clumsy efforts. There were boys as well as girls in the group, some of whom managed to pull our hair when, under duress, they were forced to dance with us.

While we cavorted on the dance floor, our Mothers sat on little gilt chairs arranged on one side of the room, while on the other side a similar row accommodated the Nannies who were there to supervise their charges. The only thing I remember liking about dancing classes was at the end of term, when we finished up with *Roger de Coverley*, a dance which gave us the opportunity to gallop up and down the two lines of the class with much abandon.

After class we changed back into our street clothes, and on special occasions had tea in the Palm Court restaurant in the hotel. This was a great treat. Sitting in the room under the potted palms, listening to the three-piece orchestral group playing the musical hits of the day, it was easy to forget the embarrassments so recently suffered in the ballroom above. As the strains of the songs from *The White Horse Inn*, *Rose Marie* and *The Desert Song* swirled round the room, even I could imagine my-self dancing gracefully at some wonderful party. White-gloved waiters offered cakes from silver stands, and the humiliations of the past hour were forgotten.

After tea we went down to Father's office to wait until he was ready to drive us home.

The firm he managed was located on the Barbican in the oldest part of the town. The cellars opened out onto the cobbles which paved all the streets down to the harbour. Across the road, the fine Victorian building which housed the Customs Office personified authority.

I used to wander into the cellars, to look at the great vats of sherry and port which stood around the walls under the curved ceiling. It was cool in the cellars, and the distant corners were cobwebby and a bit scary, but in the company of Heatly, the elderly Irishman who had been the driver there for years, fear vanished. We sat on upturned boxes and I listened to his entertaining stories of his life and times.

By the time I got to know him, he had been demoted to being a sort of general help round the firm, but previously he had been the proud driver of a pair of big bay horses which were used for deliveries.

Sadly, their day had passed, and a shiny new Ford van now took the orders round town.

Heatly had not been willing to learn to drive the van. As he confided to us, 'There's no way any God-fearing man would want to drive one of them smelly contraptions.'

As an old employee, the firm had kept him on, so he continued to keep what had been his stables neat and tidy, even polishing the brasses he had salvaged from his harness, which now hung gleaming over the door. I loved the wiry little Irishman, and was never happier than when I sat beside him and listed to his stories of his childhood in Ireland. It must have been a very poor household. They were a large family, and his Father had been a smallholder with only the sparse crops he could grow to keep them all. From a very early age, Heatly had shown a natural affinity with animals, and as soon as he left school he got a job in a local stable. The owners bred and showed riding horses, and travelled the country to shows and fairs. The boy was taken along, slept in the stables with the horses, and for a pittance and his keep, seemed to have had a happy life.

He had never married.

'I'm not really the marrying kind; the animals have been me company,' he once confided to me during one of our discussions about life.

I loved all his stories of the wonderful horses he had cared for. Easy horses, difficult horses, horses that could jump like a deer, and some that, according to him, 'Didn't have the will in them.'

I never heard him speak of a bad horse; indeed, to him there were no bad animals, only the occasional bad person.

When the War started, he enlisted in a Cavalry regiment, and for three long years looked after horses in the mud and filth of the trenches. He had survived the horrors; as he once said to me, 'I guess there wasn't a shell or bullet with me name on it'.

Occasionally he came to our home to do some work around the house or garden, and then I, and our dogs and cats, would gather round the little man to listen to his stories. He had a natural way with all living creatures, and we discussed the ways of them all. How to treat and train them. Many a time he helped me with a sick pet. He had a fund of remedies for all sorts of illness; whether it was a sick dog or a rabbit he seemed to know what to do for them. If one of my pets fell ill I relied on him to cure them, and would watch with total confidence as he put a drop of some concoction on the ear of one of my mice, or bandaged the paw which one of the dogs had cut.

When I knew him toward the end of his life, he had no animals of his own, but seemed to get great pleasure from other people's, and loved my little menagerie. I gathered that his neighbours brought their pets to him whenever they were sick. People did not have recourse to veterinary help in those days like they do now, and anyway would not have been able to afford the fees. Even in our home I never remember a vet coming to the house. We treated and nursed our animals ourselves.

I can remember my Mother sitting in front of the kitchen range with a litter of puppies abandoned by the mother, feeding them with an eye-dropper – two drops of brandy and milk every four hours. Then putting them back in a blanket-lined box under the stove for warmth. And they all survived.

I do not know what happened to Heatly, as we left Cornwall when he was still pottering about in what had been his stables, but I feel pretty sure there must be animals in his Heaven.

12. The Theatre

I THINK my lifelong passion for the theatre began with a visit to *Peter Pan*. It must have been in 1927. I looked it up in my battered old copy of *Who's Who in the Theatre* recently, and saw it was at the Garrick Theatre, and Jean Forbes-Robertson played Peter.

During the Christmas holidays of that year, we were staying with our Grandmother in St Albans, and Father decide he would take me to see the play. My elder sister had already had a theatrical treat with some friends. They had been taken to see *Where the Rainbow Ends*. This was a very popular patriotic play for children, which was put on every Winter, and I think Father thought I should have a similar treat.

Anyway, one day I was told he was going to take me to see *Peter Pan*. At tea-time Nanny dressed me in a party frock, and I was allowed to borrow my sister's velvet cloak, which since she had almost grown out of it fitted me fairly well. It made me feel very grown up, and when I was ready I went downstairs, where Father was waiting for me.

To my great surprise and delight he was in evening dress! He was carrying his opera hat – a magical piece of head-gear which one was allowed to squash flat, and it would then pop up again when you pressed the spring. I wonder if anyone has such a hat these days? Probably not, but they were a very useful item of head-gear in the days when no-one dreamed of going out without a hat in the evening. They could so easily be stowed under the theatre seat for quick retrieval at the end of the performance.

Anyway, there was Father waiting for me in the hall, and we set off for the station to take the train to London. When we arrived at St Pancras, we went to Gilbert Scott's amazing hotel building to have supper. It was, and still is, a wonderful building, and I feel glad that it has not been swept away in the post-war mania for pulling down what the Germans left us of some notable buildings in central London. We went up the great staircase to the grill-room, and were soon comfortably settled in a cosy red plush alcove from which I could survey the exciting scene of one of the busiest dining rooms in town.

I was a little apprehensive, as I had never had a meal out in the evening before, and the array of cutlery before me looked formidable. When the time came to order, I refused soup as I was not certain that I could manage the very large spoon. However, when it was suggested that I should have steak and kidney pie I felt a lot happier.

I expect Father remembered it was one of my favourite dishes and ordered it for me on that account. Anyway, it was delicious. I don't remember what followed as pudding – dessert was always a fruit course in those days – so pudding may very well have been trifle, another favourite of mine.

After we finished our meal there was a visit to the Ladies Cloakroom. Outside the door I was given a sixpence, with instructions to put it in the plate on the dressing table. This was no problem, for there was a woman in charge who helped me in a very motherly way when she understood why I was on my own.

'You are a lucky young lady, aren't you?' she said. 'Going to the theatre then, and in the evening too. I'll just tidy your hair, and you'll be all ready. Goodbye, then, enjoy yourself,' and she saw me safely outside into my Father's care.

When we got to the theatre we found our seats in the front row of the dress circle. There was a brass rail round the barrier in front of us, and in moments of great excitement I think I must have held on to it. For I never smell the scent of brass polish without being transported back to that evening and the magic of it all. When the great red curtains parted, the Darlings' nursery was revealed to my fascinated gaze. Nana, the newfoundland dog who was the children's nurse, walked across to the fireguard and picked off a garment which was being aired in front of the glow of the gas fire. Then the children were settled in bed, the lights were lowered, and Peter *flew* in through the window!

I think from that moment I was hooked on the theatre. I have had so many wonderful theatrical experiences, but few could match that particular evening.

I don't remember much more about that night. I was told I fell asleep on the train going home, and for days after I demanded that my sister should play Captain Hook to my Peter. Later, other characters began to fill the stage of my imagination, but that evening was the beginning of it all.

Serious drama did not come for many years, but pantomimes happened every year. All big towns had a Christmas pantomime, and the Theatre Royal in Plymouth was our local event. It was a different story each year, and we could never decide which we liked best. *Cinderella* or *Aladdin*? *Babes in the Wood* or *Dick Whittington*? They were all marvellous. A feature of pantomimes in those days was the transformation scene when several gauzes rose, layer after layer, to disclose Aladdin's cave with its treasure glittering in the torchlight; or the beanstalk growing up from the stage floor, higher and higher, as Jack climbed up to the castle, disappearing from view behind the proscenium arch. And perhaps our favourite of all, when the pumpkin disappeared behind a cloud of smoke and revealed the coach ready to take Cinderella to the ball, being pulled by real white ponies. There was always a comic who got the audience to shout for him when he appealed for help against the rest of the cast. There were no sophisticated songs or smutty jokes, but every year one song emerged which was the 'hit' of the year. I can remember *Yes, We Have no Bananas*, and *Tiptoe Through the Tulips*, and *The Red, Red Robin Comes Bob-bob-bobbing Along*! All of which we sang with gusto when led by Buttons or an Ugly Sister. Sometimes we went to Drury Lane. This was very special. On one such visit I fell in love with Evelyn Laye, who, as Principal Boy, was playing the Prince in a production of *Cinderella*. For the ball scene she appeared down a flight of stairs at the back of the stage, clad in canary yellow satin, and a large hat with white plumes. Sounds corny? Well, it probably was, but it was real theatre.

As we grew older, a dear maiden aunt who shared my love of the theatre took me to musicals. She was a great admirer of Ivor Novello, so we revelled in his hits. Through my childhood *The Desert Song*, *Rose Marie* and *White Horse Inn* all had long runs in the West End, and I thrilled to them all. Many years later, when we went to the opening night of *Oklahoma!* I really recaptured the thrill of a 'winner'.

13. Leaving Cornwall

MY childhood came to an abrupt end when I was thirteen.

I had already been one year at a large girls' school in Plymouth, and was finding the expanding horizons of school life, new friends and sports very much to my liking, but the village and home were still the centre of my existence.

The blow when it fell was shattering.

I had already sensed that my parents were going through a very difficult time, but in those days children were not told about adult worries. Children were not included in grown-up problems, so I had no idea of what lay in store.

Previously only the death of our beloved Grandmother had been a real disaster in my life, but that had been understandable. I knew old people had to die. Granny had been a good, kind woman, particularly to us children. She had been a Christian, and everyone knew that, in some mysterious way, good people went to Heaven when they died, so we remembered her in our prayers, and, after initial grief, accepted her disappearance from our lives.

On the day my Father told me the news we were in the greenhouse where he was working on his chrysanthemum plants, and to this day the bitter smell of the leaves as he picked them from the plants and let them fall to the floor reminds me of my incomprehension and disbelief of what he was trying to tell me.

We were going to leave Cornwall. Our house would be sold, and we would have to live in a rented home until he settled a new job.

My angry questions must have been hard for him to answer.

'How could we leave the village and the sea?'

Leaving Cornwall

'What about the animals, and where would I go to school?'

I listened to his answers in disbelief, and when he had finished ran down the path to the big pine tree and climbed up into its familiar branches and gave way to grief. The tears ran down my cheeks as I gazed out over the sea to the Eddystone lighthouse, tears of misery and rage.

The shock of leaving did not affect my sisters as much as it did me. Rosemary had already left home to take up nursing in London, and Maureen, who was only nine, was a cheerful, happy child who hardly realised what was happening. It was an adventure to her.

On the day the 'For Sale' sign went up outside the house I finally realised it was irrevocable.

Getting rid of the animals was a heart-break. The poultry went to our good neighbour and gardener, Billy Witt. Jim Pengelly became the proud owner of my white mice and guinea-pigs. The only bright spot on my horizon was that the dogs would stay with us and go wherever we lived.

As the days passed, trunks and boxes stood about half-packed in the hall and on the verandah.

I spent a lot of time sitting in my hideaway on the cliff, watching the sea, wondering what our new home would be like. I knew my parents were worried, and I could not help them so I said very little, and pretended not to care what happened.

Finally the time came for us to make our farewells.

First, to old Tom. I sat beside him on his upturned boat and explained what was happening.

He took some time to appreciate what I was saying, then he declared, 'Going to live near Lunnen, then; well that's way upalong, won't be like here, I'll be bound.'

I agreed it wouldn't; but what would it be like? I could not tell him; I had no idea myself. He said he would remember me and our trips out fishing, and I left him shaking his head over the strange way folks behaved. Why would anyone want to leave the village? Why indeed?

At the village shop, fat, red-faced Mrs Broad actually kissed me, to my acute embarrassment, and gave me a parting gift in the shape of a hideous china jug emblazoned with a crest and message 'A Gift from Cornwall'.

71

I went for a farewell tea at 'Eudora'. My best friends were the most understanding of my unhappiness. They did not tell me not to mind leaving the village, but did tell me all about the interesting things I would be able to do in a new place. The concerts I could go to, and visits to galleries and the theatre. All very well, but I would not have the sea and for that I felt there could be no consolation.

We sat and ate our saffron cake in unusual silence. Then some of my favourite records were played, and they each gave me a book as a parting gift: *The Oxford Book of English Prose* from Miss Minna, and *Kipling's Poems* from Miss Bea. Treasures which are still on my shelves today.

Finally, the day came when we were to leave. The furniture van had already lumbered away, and we all piled into Mr Greet's taxi for the journey to the station.

We drove through the village, up the hill behind Hawke's farm. As we turned the last corner the headland blocked out the sea and my childhood was over.